The
Journeyman

MAKING THE JOURNEY AND FINISHING WELL

JOHN SIPPLE

To order additional copies of this book, contact:
Bookwhip
1-855-339-3589
https://www.bookwhip.com

CONTENTS

FORWARD

May 1686

Andre Gastogne and his apprentice, Jacques, travel from their village to a neighboring village on a small cart drawn by an old dapple grey horse, six days a week. The cart has a small seat on the front, just enough room for Andre and Jacques. The rest of the cart contains the tools they need for their work as stonemasons – plus food and water for the day; oh, and a small jug of wine! Andre and his crew are in the process of building a church and the walls are about half way to the height they will be when complete…then the carpenters will come to lay timbers and planking for the roof as well as install the doors and windows that are already being built in a shop in another village.

Andre was certified as a stonemason journeyman after 3 years of apprenticing with his father, who was also a stonemason journeyman. He has been working on his own for several years and now has formed his own business and a team of nine men: two other journeyman stonemasons, each with an apprentice and 3 laborers who keep the journeyman–apprentice teams supplied with stone and other materials as needed. They have done several projects already but this is the largest. The work is hard and precision is required to assure stability of the structure, but Andre is well trained and he has assured himself that all of the people working with him are equally capable.

At the end of the day Andre and Jacques return home where dinner waits; the other men do likewise. Jacques, though not a member of the family, lives with them – room and board are his pay while apprenticing. Although they are quite tired this is the best part of the day, a time of sharing both a meal and conversation with his family and occasionally a visitor. It is well known that Andre's wife, Jacqueline, is a great cook and anyone passing through is welcome to her table to be refreshed with food and drink as well as the latest news. Both Andre and Jacqueline are Christian believers and quite involved in their village. It is also well known that both have much to offer in terms of skills and knowledge about many things. There is even talk about Andre becoming the next maire (mayor) of the village!

Journeyman: Originally from the French word "journe'e" which means a day's work or a days travel.

Eventually the word came to mean the following:

o   A man who is highly skilled in an aspect of work, with a wide range of experiences doing that work, to the point of being "certified" or recognized.
o   Responsible to supervise younger men (apprentices) and teach them all aspects of the trade/craft.
o   Capable of working unsupervised themselves and also to become "self employed"; ie, start their own business.
o   The very capable "journeyman" is loyal, as a husband, father, and friend - known to be a man you can "count on" to lend a helping hand.
o   Note: the story about Andre is fiction: based on the above description of a Journeyman.

My first encounter with the word journeyman was my first job with DuPont's construction division, which built the large chemical plant facilities that produced their products. The people doing the construction work belonged to construction building trade unions such as pipefitters, electricians, carpenters, ironworkers, etc. My wife Kathie and I became friends with an older couple named Bill and Jeanie. He was an Ironworker superintendent and she a housewife mom. They were in their 60's and we were 22 - They took us under their wing. He taught me the ropes regarding construction and she helped with the arrival of our first child Kim.

Bill was a horse of a man yet gentle and pleasant to be around. When asked how he was doing he would respond with a big grin and the words, "If it was any better I couldn't stand it!" He cared for his men and they cared for him. In the construction business, work comes and goes so there is a bit of a 'revolving door' regarding workers (tradesmen). Many superintendents treated this like they had been treated coming up through the ranks – like cattle.

Bill was different; he treated them like he would want to be treated – with respect as a fellow man. When he had to let a man go he didn't just tell them to hit the road, he took them to his office and told them how much he appreciated them and the work they had done. He would tell them he was sorry that the work was finished and that they had to leave (in a union situation that meant they returned to the union hall to find out where they would be assigned to next). There was a system for it but Bill went out of his way to show care and appreciation for them – he respected them as men and as skilled craftsman. Then he would shake their hand and say something like, "see you soon I hope!" I heard someone say that Bill was the only craft superintendent he had ever seen who could fire a man and have him (the craftsman) say 'thank you' when he left.

Bill was a true leader of men but he was also a 'journeyman'. He went through the years of apprenticeship process himself to develop the skills to become a journeyman ironworker before he was allowed to work unsupervised and then to become a supervisor himself. In fact, he was so good at it that he became the overall superintendent for all ironwork* in the construction process. Bill paid attention to people as well as the technology of building. He was a student of people and understood how to care for them as well as manage them and the process they worked on. As a result he and his team were simply more productive and quality

---

* All ironwork would primarily mean the basic structure of the building

conscious than most. He was well known and men were thrilled to be assigned to a project being supervised by Bill.

After DuPont I worked for several years in manufacturing environments - the word Journeyman wasn't used but the concept was present. I have observed that ten to twenty percent of workers are natural thought leaders - they have a capability of influencing others in their way of thinking. Typically these individuals also have high technical capability, important in their ability to influence others.

This is an important thing to understand regarding the development of organizational capability. To accomplish anything, whether it's a change or something new, you must win the support of these thought leaders to be successful. Without this support any effort is likely to not succeed. Actually, this is true in all life situations where people are involved – the success of anything begins with leadership agreeing, We all know that but what is often missed is that *leadership also includes these thought leaders that exist throughout an organization.*

I also believe that a journeyman's character extends beyond the vocational arena to the family, community and faith aspects of life – or should. It's no guarantee, of course, but many of these men, because of the character development to become a journeyman, also become successful in many of the things they touch in life, which ultimately leads to a reality of "finishing well" their life journey overall.

What about women – does this journeyman concept apply to them?

The term "journeyman" seems specifically to focus on men – there is no word like it for women – like Journeywoman. There is no doubt, however, that there is a complementary way of thinking about women. Women historically have followed a kind of apprenticeship model as daughters learn from their mothers, grandmothers, and other women, the same concept as men but for different kinds of things – but this is highly blurred. Many of the same characteristics would be present, the journeyman model is focused primarily on vocational skills but for women it would likely have more aspects of people/family relationships.

4

Certainly in my own experience I saw equal levels of the Journeyman characteristic for women in my family: My mother and my grandmother each had significant roles in the family business, both in terms of craft skills and business skills. I also had a great aunt who took over a fairly large manufacturing business when her husband died and managed it very well for a number of years before turning it over to a son. And then, in my own family, my wife and I have three daughters, one a teacher, another a nurse practitioner, and the third has partnered with my son in law to start up two businesses. I've also had the privilege of working with many competent women over the years in the corporate world and through my consulting practice.

One can't help but think of the many stories about mothers and grandmothers who support and raise a family by themselves after losing their husband to war, accident, or just leaving, etc. Occasionally, we see a young individual receiving an award or commendation of some sort, pay tribute to his mother, or a grandmother, who have raised their family as a single parent.

Since the dictionary only has the word 'journeyman' I think it's appropriate to do the American thing and invent a new word: 'journeywoman'. Another perhaps more descriptive term comes to mind however...*Wonder woman!* I know there is a "superhero" character with this name, but the wonder woman I'm thinking about is real, she is my wife, my mother, my daughters who are now moms. She is that unsung hero that does whatever is needed and then some to raise her children, her grandchildren and then help some others less fortunate than they, and she is that capable leader that is the heart and soul of any variety of enterprises. Those are the true *wonder women*.

Journeymen like Bill and Andre and journeywomen like my wife, daughters and my aunt Louise are very important to our culture - they have played a major role in the story of America; but now, they seem to be vanishing. The original leaders of our country emerged from people like this, citizen representatives in government, teachers in education, leaders in business and every part of our society. We must encourage a return of this role in our culture…it has been so important throughout our history as a country – both in terms of the health and welfare of families and communities as well as national interests, like defending our country, helping to rebuild after a storm, or fire, or any number of other situations that simply require others to come alongside and lead by lending a hand.

PART I

CHAPTER 1

JOURNEYMEN: WHO ARE THEY?

They are everywhere but not everyone, in fact they are about 15% of any population of men. They are not always noticeable but are sometimes very noticeable. They are the guy that shows up to help, the guy that has a valuable word of advice, the guy that shares his stuff, the guy that really knows how to do something, the guy who, when he speaks others shush up and listen, the guy you can count on for most anything when you most need help.

On a team, he is the guy who seems to be the "spark-plug", everything works when he is there and it doesn't when he is not.

When a journeyman dies, everyone shows up for the celebration of his life and says, "we're really gonna miss him"!

Lloyd Henry was a journeyman. He didn't know he was and it was never his objective; but as one reviews his life he surely was one! It might have had something to do with his father, the way he raised Lloyd – on a small farm in upstate New York. In the 1930's there were many small farms all over the country, the "Big Box" mentality was still a ways off. There were many different kinds of things a boy growing up could do on a small farm: land to work and plant, crops to cultivate and harvest, farm machinery to take care of, animals to care for, produce to take to market, farm hands to manage in certain seasons, and so on. Caring for a small herd of milk cows was a twice a day responsibility 365 days a year – they had to be milked and there were no milking machines then, you did it literally by hand.

And in between, when you could find the time there was always more to do – a tractor that needed an oil change or a new tire, a section of roof on the barn that needed to be replaced, a plan for next year developed, supplies to be purchased, customers to be located for the produce of the farm, and, hopefully, money to be managed - and bills to be paid.

It was a busy lifestyle and a farmer had to be "multi-skilled" to do it. Lloyd Henry, like all youngsters growing up on a farm, was multi-skilled by age ten plus he was a "tinkerer". One of his favorite things to do was to tear apart something, anything really, to see what was inside, how it worked; and then put it back together…well, most of the time. He built a boat when he was fifteen and he and a friend replaced an old truck's transmission when he was seventeen. It worked pretty good when they were done except it went backwards when it was supposed to go forward and forward when it was supposed to go backward. So they had to do it over – but they learned. They learned two things; they learned how to fix a transmission but the more important lesson was they learned not to give up – to complete what they had started out to do. On a farm, at a pretty young age you learn what to do…and what not to do.

The farm Lloyd grew up on was quite small, 30 acres; too small to be a dairy farm. So, Lloyd went to an agriculture & technology two-year college to study farm machinery repair. He learned all he needed in one year and went home to marry his high school sweet heart and start a business. Very few farms at that time had tractors, hay bailing machines or grain combines, but the farmers did grow hay to feed the milk cows and they also raised wheat or oats or both. It was Lloyd's idea to buy that equipment and bale hay and combine the grain for them. Lloyd and his father bought two *Farmall* tractors, two *International Harvester* bailing machines and an *International Harvester* Combine. (A machine that cuts the stalks of wheat or oats, etc., combines them together, takes off the grain at their tops and combines them together in a bag or in a large tank on the back of another truck that follows alongside. That was the beginning of their business to help local farmers harvest their crops.

This wasn't the only business they formed, there was also a business to build and install truck bodies. Farmers typically bought a truck with no body behind the cab – just the back end of the truck frame to which the rear axel and wheels were attached. Farmers reasoned they could build the body for the truck and most of them could. Lloyd figured that if he could build a really good body for not too much money the farmers would likely buy them. It worked, and that business succeeded for several years.

The story doesn't end here. Perhaps the centerpiece of this small farm was a small maple syrup operation. Going back to Lloyd's father, he had learned to make the syrup on a little farm located on a small mountain where he grew up in the Catskills Mountains of upstate New York.

In the 1940's they began to increase the size of the maple syrup operation though tapping maple trees on the properties of all those farmers they had baled hay and combined wheat and oats for…and probably built a truck body and perhaps a hay wagon for. By the 1950's it had become a serious business and as the truck body business faded away it became the main enterprise on the farm.

Lloyd was doing what he was created for and prepared to do. It was as if all the years and experiences leading up to this was "for just such a time as this". He was a "journeyman", not in a certified way but in a life experience sort of way that is true for many men. He knew how to do a lot of things, from welding, to woodworking to electrical systems. He knew enough to know he could learn how to do anything. He applied this to the maple business in ways that caught the attention of others. He invented a way to finish the final stage of evaporating the water with steam heat instead of oil or wood, which could burn the syrup or leave a strange taste. This required a steam boiler and he found an old one, refurbished it and adapted it to his process. He also invented machines to make maple cream and sugar candies; many of these machines are still in service.

The maple production season was February to April when the maple trees were coming out of dormancy and the sap was beginning to rise. People came to the farm in carloads to see this ancient art made modern (the Indians made maple syrup before any Europeans arrived). Lloyd, seeing the interest level rising decided to create a newsletter about the Maple industry – and called it *The Maple Digest*. He wrote most of it and published it for distribution to a growing list of interested people. For years it was the main information forum in the small industry (Maple syrup is produced in the US Northeast, the upper Midwest, and eastern Canada. This is where "sugar maples" grow).

His own business grew to 5000 gallons a year, which required 200,000 gallons of maple sap from several thousand maple trees* to be evaporated. 40 gallons of sap were required for each gallon of syrup so 39 gallon of water had to go through a process of evaporation in huge pans heated from below (originally wood fires, then oil fires, finally, in Lloyd's case, steam running through coils in the evaporator pans). Though it all sounds impressive – and it was impressive - it was still a small family owned business, big relative to others both in terms of output of syrup and especially ideas.

One of the most interesting projects Lloyd took on was a technique called *reverse osmosis,* which was being developed to pull fresh water out of seawater. Scientists in a Federal agriculture lab in Philadelphia as well as professors and researchers at Cornell university and the University of Vermont were trying to find a way to adapt the process to maple syrup production – in effect to pull the water out of the maple sap leaving syrup or at least sap with a greater concentration of sugar so that the

---

* Depending on the size of the tree – some would produce a quart of syrup to 2 quarts for the bigger trees.

evaporation process could be faster and use less fuel. They needed a place to test their hypothesis and asked Lloyd if they could come to his farm and set up a little lab space there. He was all for it and not only provided the space but jumped in himself to help.

Now this is interesting! A farmer with a one-year agricultural school education in farm machinery repair, joining a team of PhD's, professors and researchers from the US extension lab in Philadelphia, Cornell University and the University of Vermont to figure out how to apply something called *reverse osmosis* to the making of maple syrup. Well, he did have a maple syrup operation and had offered space for them to work, but who would think he would or could take it any further than that. Well, he could and he did! Turns out, in addition to everything else he'd learned over the years he wasn't too bad at chemistry either.

This is a real story about a real person. Lloyd Henry's last name is Sipple and he is my father… A Journeyman raised me and that is what now motivates me to write this book. Also, it has guided me in my own journey and caused me to observe and appreciate the Journeymen I've encountered - it's like I've lived the research needed for this book.

CHAPTER 2

BIBLICAL JOURNEYMEN

The Bible provides several examples of Journeymen and the end of the book of Proverbs is a wonderful chapter written about women: "The Wife of Nobel Character" Also known as "The Proverbs Woman". I love the chapter and what it says about women but I'm writing about Journeymen. I wish there was a chapter about "The Proverbs Man". There isn't specifically but as I read the book of Proverbs it is clear that much is said to and about men – so I have taken the liberty to pull out specific things and organize them into themes to provide a picture of what the "Proverbs Man" might look like.

The proverbs man has decided to "trust in the Lord with all his heart, and not lean on his own understanding; in everything he does he acknowledges the Lord knowing that only he can make his path straight" *(paraphrase of Proverbs 3, 5-6)*. He has decided to allow the Lord to guide him in the way of wisdom and to apply his heart to seeking wisdom over all else, which leads to the development of his character in the areas of integrity, humility, generosity, care and development of others, and work. The end result is power, wealth, and success - but not <u>of</u> the world, lasting at best for a life time; rather <u>in</u> the Lord and lasting eternally.

The Proverbs man "obtains favor from the Lord" 12:2

He will experience "…a straight path; when he walks he will not be hampered; and when he runs he will not stumble." 3:5-6

He will experience a result "more precious than rubies, and nothing he could desire "can compare…" 8:11

His "wife of noble character" will be his "crown" 12:4

He will have "great power…increased strength…" 24: 5,6

He will "bring joy to his father." 29:3

His…"plans will succeed" 16:3

He "will prosper; for he refreshes others…" 11:25

He will be "kept safe" for he "trusts in the Lord" 29:25

He will have "abundant food" because he is diligent in his work. 12:11 and 28:19

He will "be blessed for he shares his food with the poor" 22:9

He will experience a crown of "children's children" in his later years. 17:6

A full presentation of my summarizing effort can be found in the addendum.

Biblical Journeymen (Proverbs Men):

Joseph (Genesis 37; 39-50)
The youngest of Jacob's sons, Joseph, was sold into slavery by his brothers to a caravan heading to Egypt. There he was placed in the service of the captain of the Pharaoh's guard. He found favor quickly and was put in charge of the captain's household. From there he encountered several difficult obstacles beginning with harassment from the captain's wife but persevered through all of it with his dignity and reputation intact;

that plus his diligence and excellence in the work assigned him, caught the eye of important and powerful people. This allowed him to be promoted and eventually he became the second most powerful person in all of Egypt, as well as an important link in the overall story of the development of the nation of Israel.

The story of Joseph is thought provoking. He role modeled what it takes to become a journeyman. Life always has it's ups and downs, and while most of us don't experience the magnitude of what Joseph experienced, his story does encourage us to never give in and to never give up – one never knows what perseverance will lead to but there is a verse of scripture that says it will at least lead to the development of our character and from that to hope, and hope doesn't disappoint us. (Paraphrased from Romans 5: 3-5)

Caleb (Numbers 14 and Joshua 14)
Then there is the story of Caleb *(Numbers 14 and Joshua 14)*; who, along with Joshua, were the only Israelites to have the faith and courage to cross over the Jordan River to the Promised Land. All the others believed it couldn't be done. Because of this faithfulness, God promised Caleb a portion of good land when they got there; but it took 45 years for that to finally come about.

Nothing is written about those 45 years and what it took for Caleb and Joshua to persevere that long, but they did it and this is what Celeb had to say at the end of it, *"So, here I am today, eighty five years old! I am just as strong today as the day Moses sent me out…now let me have this hill country the Lord promised me that day. You heard that the Anakites are there and their cities are large and fortified, but, with the Lord helping me, I will drive them out just as he said." (Joshua: 14,10-12).*

What I find interesting about Caleb is the 45 years he waited for his dream, talk about perseverance! We can only imagine what that must have been like, my guess is that he didn't just lay around – he made himself busy, he found things that needed to be done, people to coach, whatever, and whatever he did he did well. That is a mark of a Journeyman.

Nehemiah (Nehemiah)
One of my favorite examples is Nehemiah, the governor who organized the rebuilding of Jerusalem in 432 B.C. Every effort to rebuild the ruined city failed until Nehemiah was appointed governor by the Babylonian king Artaxerxes.

What he did was simple and brilliant. The walls of the city had been knocked down and the massive gates reduced to ashes. This allowed their enemies to ransack the city at will. Nehemiah gave the residents of Jerusalem a mission: "Come, let us rebuild the walls and we will no longer be in disgrace!"

Certainly this wasn't the first time anyone considered this. What they lacked was an effective plan. Nehemiah had one. His plan was for each family to rebuild the portion of the wall next to their house and for shopkeepers to do the same. He had the priests rebuild the sheep gate—special to them because that was the gate they primarily used. In other words, he asked people to concentrate on rebuilding where they had a personal stake.

You might be thinking, *that's an interesting story but what does it have to do with Journeymen?*

Here is the beginning of the story: Nehemiah was born into captivity. He was slave and developed for service to the king. Someone he respected and from whom he could learn likely tutored him in a way that would cause him to become highly capable and find favor with the king. Like many cultures in slavery, the Jewish culture would have done all they could to preserve their ways, so whether or not parents were involved with young Nehemiah, someone was there to teach him.

What did they teach? They would have taught from historical writings available as well as practical life skills a young man or woman needed. Like our culture in America, the Jews of that time had a rich heritage in the form of what is now the old testament of the Bible. Stories of leaders like Abraham, Joseph, Moses, Joshua, David and Daniel, would have provided much for a young lad to think about—just as we learn from more recent great leaders such as Washington, Lincoln, Churchill, Martin Luther King, and Ronald Reagan.

The combination of stories about earlier leaders, who not only survived slavery but excelled to the point of becoming top leaders in those foreign cultures, probably prepared Nehemiah in terms of his worldview—and the resulting beliefs, attitudes, and assumptions that made up who he was - this is where the development of heart and character would have started for Nehemiah and from this heart and character developed a man, a Journeyman who was able to accomplish all that he accomplished – in his first go at being a leader.

Cornelius, the Centurion *(Acts 10)*
Cornelius lived in Caesarea, Judea, around the time of Christ and was a Centurion in the Roman Army. I investigated what it meant, to be a Centurion and learned some interesting things. First, unlike most leaders throughout history who received their positions as a result of being a member of the upper class or the nobility, men became centurions as a result of what they did as a soldier...a legionnaire! They were chosen as a result of their physical size and strength and their dexterity and expertise with weapons and fighting along with character traits such as vigilance, even temperament, quickness to execute and take action, and bravery. In effect, they were promoted from the rank and file, based on what they had demonstrated over time in the way of both skill and character.

Once in the role of being a Centurion, they were expected to lead "from the front", and to "set an example" for their soldiers to follow. They were also expected to "exercise and maintain proper discipline among their soldiers...maintaining cleanliness, being properly dressed, and maintaining their weapons - making sure they were "well rubbed and bright". Doing this well along with evidence of "conspicuous bravery" could lead to promotion as a Centurion, to a level of being responsible for other Centurions and their soldiers.

I can imagine a young man aspiring to be a centurion much like young men today aspire to be a warrior in our military, or an athlete playing a competitive sport, or aspiring to learn a craft like their father and build a business from it. Perhaps Cornelius was one of these young men and he aspired to be a soldier and fight great battles of great importance and one day, perhaps, to become a Centurion in the great Roman army. This may have been his dream and nothing else mattered.

So, he did it and he became not only a Centurion; but, a really great man, it seems. The only account we have of this man is in the tenth chapter of Acts, From it we can guess at a little more of what kind of man he became…*"At Caesarea there was a man named Cornelius, a centurion in what was known as the Italian Regiment. He and all his family were devout and God-fearing; he gave generously to those in need and prayed to God regularly."* (Acts 10: 1-2). Not only was Cornelius a Centurion, he was a family man, had become "God fearing", plus he was generous and interested in helping others.

This is not a small thing, in those times the Romans were not particularly fond of this new movement started by a man called Jesus. The Romans worshiped pagan gods and considered Christians to be atheists. They were all about power and control, more interested in what they could achieve personally than helping others. It was a powerful empire and as powerful empires have come and gone throughout history; they took what they wanted and destroyed the rest. Cornelius had risen to a level of influence in that system but he had also grown as a man in other important areas of life. As he became "God fearing " he also became a man of prayer and in a prayer time he had a vision of an angel who said to him, *"Your prayers and gifts to the poor have come up as a memorial offering before God. Now send men to Joppa to bring back a man who is called Peter." (Acts 10: 4-5)*

So Cornelius sent three men to find Peter, who was one of the twelve Jesus picked to train and who were now leading the new movement following Christ in Jerusalem. When they meet Peter they said to him, *"We have come from Cornelius the Centurion, he is a righteous and God fearing man, who is respected by all the Jewish people" (Acts 10: 22).* They then explained Cornelius' request for him to come to Caesarea. Peter went and was invited to speak to a group assembled by Cornelius. The topic was to be Jesus and the power of the Holy Spirit. The result of this was that all who were assembled received the gift of the Holy Spirit and were baptized.

It is not my intention to unpack all of this spiritually; my interest is in Cornelius the Centurion…the Journeyman. We don't know exactly how he started in life but we do know that he became a Centurion, he trained for it, he worked for it, he proved himself able to be one… someone recognized that and promoted him to it. Along with that he became a family man, and he did well enough to have a following of younger men and a household of people who probably cooked his food, kept his property in good shape, etc. Also, along the way, he became "God fearing", and if that means anything like it does today, he emptied himself of himself to accept a "higher power", and then he reached out to someone more learned than him about this new faith, to come and teach himself and the people in his household…his circle of influence. Actually, this was the first time Peter ever spoke to a non-Jewish group, so Cornelius was a catalyst for the movement of the gospel of Jesus Christ in the early world along with Peter, Paul and all the rest.

CHAPTER 3

JOURNEYMEN IN THE WORK PLACE

My own experience in several different work places around the country includes knowing many journeymen, and observing their character and capabilities first hand. In my younger years several, like Bill, the ironwork superintendent in the forward, personally coached me.

I could list many more names and tell stories of each but I'll limit it to just one. His name is Fred and he was a kind of journeyman's journeyman. He was so good in what he did, both technically and interpersonally that all who knew him – or knew of him – would immediately accept what Fred said or suggested as being right. In his mid sixties he had developed a reputation of being very strong technically and very willing to share his knowledge. We realized that this knowledge was contained only in Fred so we began an effort to get it out of him and into a form to be useful. We began to record question and answer sessions as a way to save the valuable information. Unfortunately, within a few years the business was sold, a new company took over and the information that we had filed away was lost.

As I think about this now, this has happened to virtually every Journeyman that has walked on this earth with very few exceptions like those written about in the Bible. The reality is that they are here for a season, they make their contribution – quite an important contribution for the most part…and then they are gone and in most cases forgotten. For many years in this country, and probably others, the talents and capabilities were passed along to the next generation but the reality at this point of the 21st century is that even this is lost as electronic and virtual approaches, with very few people if any, are substituted.

Layer of Opportunity –The Backbone

So what would a journeyman or journeywoman have to offer in this day and age? I believe there is a *layer of opportunity* in every culture. It is a thin layer in the population of people that is often missed or at least not understood. Actually, it is one of the top layers along with "senior leaders"; i.e., Presidents, CEOs, senior managers, top government officials (Governors, Senators, Congressmen/women, Judges) and the very wealthy. This level is positioned at the very top and typically, is responsible for policy and strategy; ie, **what** will be done. How they get to the top is multifaceted ranging from inheritance to election and sometimes, but not typically, it is earned. The primary problem with all of this is that they typically don't know **how** to do what they envision.

There is a layer just below comprised of highly capable individuals who actually do most of the leading of the actual work and activity necessary to accomplish anything and it is this layer that we are labeling as **journeymen and women.** A characteristic of this level in our culture is that they don't tend to "toot their horn" much, but the truth is that without this layer senior leaders would, for the most part, fail.

This layer emerges naturally. My observation after working with hundreds of teams over 50 years is that for every ten individuals there are one or two – about 15%* -that have leadership capability and the initiative to do something with that capability. They will lead whether

---

* Recent studies on the value of *normal distribution* thinking and a concept called *Power distribution* (indicate source – articles in Harvard Business Review, Forbes, etc).

or not you tell them to and not always in the direction you want them to go…but they will lead. They are born with it, it may not be polished but they are influencers and can make something happen, be it a revolt or a championship.

Perhaps a better way to describe the layer is the word "backbone". Each of us has a backbone, without it we could not stand or do anything really. It is the basis of our physical human body. *It isn't the head, but the head sits on it, it isn't the heart but the heart is protected by it, and it isn't the body, but the body structure is connected to it. Organizationally, the head is leadership, and also the place where all the important information is kept – in the brain. The heart is where the core values, principles, characteristics, and understanding of whom we are and why we are here reside. The body is the organization that functions to accomplish the actions determined by the heart and the head.*

For this to work there must be an order and function for each part; so, organizationally, the first and most important structural part of the body is the *backbone.* Leaders can envision, the brain can hold all kinds of wonderful information, the heart can cause us to know right from wrong, but nothing can really happen until it is deployed and acted on; without the backbone that would not be possible!

The backbone is what I am identifying as journeymen and journeywomen, the layer that emerges as "key people", who can and do influence others. They are people who can "think outside the box", take initiative, and make something happen. They are people you can count on to *be there* – "dressed and ready to play", to quote a phrase often used with athletes. This backbone has been evident for the 400 years of our history; America wouldn't be America without it.

To illustrate this allow me to tell a story. Richard was a member of an organization we were trying to re-organize; it was dysfunctional and incapable of reaching the goals and targets that "senior management" wanted. Our approach was to invite the workers to "be part of the solution" instead of part of the problem! We began by recruiting a cross organizational team of 35 people: managers, union leaders, technicians, and general workers. Richard was one of the individuals who volunteered. We knew that he had strong opinions and that he could dominate a conversation and not listen much to others.

As we started he was indeed very opinionated but he soon surprised us and began to listen more to the ideas of others. The conversations were lively as each debated their points. As the process progressed, Richard became smoother in his approach, more willing to listen to other opinions and ideas and would adjust his opinion when it made sense. The net result was that Richard grew in his ability to work with others; he was thoughtful and considerate and ultimately turned into one of the key leaders of the effort we were promoting.

Eventually he became a role model and spokesperson for others, a key person in influencing others to adopt the changes needed. Indeed, as the process continued several others also became thought leaders and together led an overall effort that converted a thousand-person organization to think differently about how to do the work. The overall change effort was highly successful. The organization pulled together and created a synergism not normally seen in large manufacturing organizations. The bottom line was an overall improvement to the results of the business that reduced our costs by almost 30%, which in turn increased the bottom line from barely break even to an annual return of over 20% (EBITA – earnings before interest, taxes, amortization).

As I continued my own journey from the Cottage business my grandfather and father started, to the corporate world of large organizations and finally on to the information age and the proliferation of organizations large and small, I have noticed one thing regarding organizational health – the strongest are clearly those that have recognized and empowered the journeymen and journeywomen to do what they can do!

My contention is that this layer of journeymen/women, like Richard, emerged in all walks of life in America – business, military, communities, etc. In the fantastic story that is the founding and development of our country, this was the "backbone" that enabled it. Of course there were the great American leaders like *Washington, Franklin, Lincoln, King, and the inventors like Franklin, Edison, Ford, the Wright brothers, Albert Einstein* ... who set a direction; but it was this backbone that pulled it off, that got on the small, sailing ships to sail to this country, that had the courage to travel westward in a wagon, that built a small business around their craft. This backbone enabled the dream, the vision to become reality. They are the ones who led and did the hard work that resulted in.....*America!*

America, The Beautiful

Oh beautiful for spacious skies,
For amber waves of grain
For purple mountain majesties
Above the fruited plane

America, America! God shed is grace on thee
And crown thy good with <u>brotherhood</u>,
From sea to shining sea!

Oh beautiful for pilgrim feet
Whose stern impassion'd stress
A thoroughfare for <u>freedom</u> beat
Across the wilderness!

America! America! God mend thine ev'ry flaw,
Confirm thy soul in self control,
Thy <u>liberty</u> in law!

Oh beautiful for <u>heroes proved</u>
In liberating strife,
<u>Who more than self their country loved,</u>
And mercy more than life!

America! America! May God thy gold refine
Till all success be nobleness,
And ev'ry gain devine

Oh beautiful for <u>patriot dream</u>
That sees beyond the years
Thine alabaster cities gleam,
Undimmed by human tears!

America! America!; <u>God shed His grace on thee,</u>
And crown they good with brotherhood
From sea to shining sea!

PART II

CHAPTER 4

AMERICA THE BEAUTIFUL: WHAT HAPPENED?

Sweet land of liberty, brotherhood, the hope of the world…what has happened to it all. Our country is supposed to be a society in which the people are involved in the leadership and direction of the country, '*Government of the people, by the people, for the people*', to quote Abraham Lincoln (Gettysburg address, 1863). All individuals can aspire to and become whatever or whomever they wish… perhaps even a celebrity – in theory at least. Practically speaking of course, only a very small percentage actually become celebrities; CEO's: presidents, elected officials, famous athletes, entertainers, wealthy entrepreneurs, etcetera. What I find interesting…and perplexing…is that today, we as a society seem fixated on celebrities, as if they are the role models we should follow in order to accomplish the "American Dream" and collect our share of the pie.

There was a time in our history when our role models reflected the values and virtues of this newly discovered continent and the country that was established, The United States of America. Those values and virtues were things like: hard work, determination, perseverance, honesty and integrity, neighborliness and respect for each other. Following their lead made sense.

Today, however, most celebrities seem focused on themselves, how wonderful they are and what they can do to further their personal aspirations. That isn't true of all, of course, but I believe it is true of many, enough to significantly affect how our younger generations, who are taking their queues from these folks - how they think and behave. Another reality seems to be that although celebrities have their time of achievement and glory, many really don't finish well. Moral failures, marital unfaithfulness, cheating, and bankruptcy (both monetarily and relationally) become an Achilles tendon that ruptures and stops their journey before they reach the finish line.

For those who allow themselves to be influenced by these pampered role models, their finish is often messed up as well. We can identify entire portions of our American society, which are at least badly blighted by this and some pockets where there is little hope at all for the American Dream or anything else for that matter. Supporting systems to enable the preparation of our young people – schools, information age tools, government programs, etc. – have become ineffective and actually counter productive.

When was the last time you saw kids in a park playing basketball or just running around and playing games they created on their own? When has a young man held a door for you as you entered a building, how many hats are off when our National anthem is played, or an invocation given? How many high school students do you know who have a part time job? What about the statistics that rate our emerging generation's readiness to take on adulthood, relative to other countries? We are way down the list in many areas. Universities are now recommending that high school graduates take a "gap year" before going to college; because many are simply not ready. (The idea is for them to mature a bit by working and learning a skill, or an educational trip to see and learn about another culture, or mission oriented travel to participate in a project to help others, etc.).

Then there are the statistics regarding the family; divorce rates, single parent homes, drug and alcohol abuse, rape...and on it goes.

There are exceptions to all of this, of course, but it seems like a trend that is going in the wrong direction and getting worse. What has happened to the American Dream? What has happened to America? I'm not convinced that just trying harder will get us anywhere – if the system we are working with is the problem - and it surely must be - then **it is doubtful that we can change the result unless we change the system.** There is an old adage that working on the same thing over and over again and expecting a different result is insanity, or it will surely lead to that end.

Allow me to Digress!

A primary impetus in the American story was people coming in a quest for what they called religious freedom. They felt smothered by "old world" religious institutions, which allowed little freedom to worship and follow God the way they wished. This was not a new thing really; after all, this was the 1600's and 16 hundred years before that there was a religious institution called the Pharisees who blocked, for a time, the message brought to the people by a man named Jesus. He claimed to be the son of God and that caused the Pharisees a real problem because after a thousand years or so of working out every jot and tittle of their religious system they felt like they had it all figured out. So, Jesus and his growing band of followers just didn't fit.

Well, you probably know the story – if you don't you should 'Google' it for sure, it's amazing! They killed him is what they did… end of problem! Except it wasn't! First of all He didn't die (that's another story) and those followers just kept on…for the next 1600 years or so until the beginning of the American story, and that story begins in England where the first tiny group of people came from…searching for religious freedom. No, the Pharisees were not in England but through the centuries men and women have either brought forward old ways of thinking about religion or created their own version.

It all seems to do with one rather difficult human element to explain. See, right in the beginning (the beginning as told in the Bible), there is this verse: *Then God said, Let us make mankind in our image, in our likeness…So God created mankind in his own image…male and female he created them. God blessed them and said to them, "be fruitful and increase in number; fill the earth and subdue it".* (Genesis 1:27, 28)

In another place about the creation of the first man and woman it says this: *"but, for Adam no suitable helper was found. So God caused the man to fall asleep and while he was sleeping he took one of the man's ribs and then closed up the place with flesh. Then he made a woman from the rib he had taken out of the man and he brought her to the man. The man said, "This is now bone of my bones and flesh of my flesh: she shall be called " woman' for she was taken out of man".* It goes on to say, *"For this reason a man leaves his father and mother and is united to his wife, and they become one flesh".* (Genesis 2: 20-24)

So, this is the beginning of the problem, or the solution, depending on your point of view regarding life. What I mean is there have always been people who have embraced this story and the rest of God's story as told in the Bible – especially the story of Jesus, which is contained in what is called the New Testament portion of the Bible. Those who know this story, know that a most amazing gift is contained, the gift of forgiveness and eternal life. These are the people who have always searched for a place to live and build their lives according to the promises of God – also contained throughout the Bible.

But there have also been people who have never heard the story or who have refused to accept it as true. Depending on how many believe versus those who don't has everything to do with the culture of a Nation, a community, a family, or a person.

Coming back to the America story, a group called "Pilgrims" first settled the continent and many others followed who had a similar belief system. This is not to say that all who came 'believed' in Jesus, but many did and it set a course regarding the development of a culture, unlike anything in the world at that time. That culture guided those who developed the constitution of the United States, which became a very successful national culture…recognized, and admired, around the world. For the first 200 years of our nations history this was the prevailing culture and it focused on things like:

- Belief in God: Father, Son and Holy Spirit
- A character of love, forgiveness, service, respect for human life, and dignity for all people
- A life style focused on the above along with hard work to provide for the needs of a family

This national culture became strong enough to win wars, yet kind and generous enough to help the nations who lost to regain the ground they had lost. It has been a culture that has created the most amazing technical discoveries and also achieved a level of wealth never before seen or known – and shared it with others. A culture in which you didn't have to lock your doors – you trusted your neighbors because they were your friends and you knew if someone tried to come against you from outside, they would be there to help. In fact it remains as the one culture in the world where all turn out to help in a time of need, like a catastrophic storm or similar horrific event – and not only for its own people but also for the people of nations around the world. It has been a culture in which anyone can realize his or her dream, and it has been a culture to which many from other nations have come to find a better life and realize their dream.

Some would say this isn't true because they haven't realized their dream. Certainly the culture doesn't guarantee it, and it does take personal initiative to start, to stick to a plan, probably a lot of hard work, and often a failure or several failures along the way. It takes perseverance to stay with it and not give up, to try a different path perhaps, and, it may take adaptability to adjust the target or the path to get to the target, to something that fits better with gifts and capabilities and current circumstances.

But, it has always been possible, to literally achieve anything and there are many stories of individuals who started with nothing, which in the "old world" would have absolutely prevented success; but they rose above it in this new American culture and achieved much. What we perhaps miss are the stories of Journeymen and Journeywomen who accomplished much with their life, not celebrity status perhaps, but much in the way of a contribution to a family, to a business, a church, a community, etc. Think about all who died protecting our nation, or those who faithfully performed their tasks as part of building a great business, or those who poured into their children or students and provided them with a dream as well as the skills to achieve it. Oh, there has always been opportunity in this great nation, for those willing to do whatever is needed (legally and ethically) to achieve it.

Going back to the question, what has happened to America? I can only give you my belief (although I know it is widely held by others). I believe we, as a nation, a multicultural nation, have 'lost our way'. As time has gone on, as more and more 'other' cultures have formed, and more generations have come along, they have brought different ways of thinking and behaving...we have become more diverse and multicultural (which should be a good thing), *without a clear vision and set of clear values/principles to guide us.*

Please don't misunderstand, I am in favor of diversity and multiculturalism – I saw it thrive in my days of leading large organizations – but it was always built on a set of common values and directed toward a common vision. I believe that describes the United States for 200 years: the vision was to provide a place where every individual could grow and become who God made them to be...in safety, and a set of core values were clearly spelled out in our national constitution and system of laws.

I further believe this is being eroded as I write this (2019). Our government processes have become increasingly obscure in trying to micromanage our lives and yet doing little to address the world issues that could eventually, "eat our lunch".

At the heart of this, in my mind, is the replacement of the people who were our role models a generation ago with celebrities who are mostly interested in achieving their own end, whatever it is.

And just to take it a bit further, I believe that the Journeymen and Journeywomen, are left on the sidelines. The leaders of today have no idea of what this means and what is lost by not having them "on the field" playing the role they have capability to play. Without this aspect of society – this "backbone" layer - and the capability it provides, the leaders of today cannot and will not be successful; and by the time they realize it, if they ever do – it may well be too late!

CHAPTER 5

LESSONS FROM HISTORY

Many are saying, "We have lost our way". Perhaps before focusing on where we want our country to go we should review a bit of history. We don't want to go backwards, but the reality might be that there are some good things in our American history that we should consider…and perhaps retrieve for the future, or remember not to do again!

The first Americans fascinate me, both those we call "native Americans" and those who first immigrated to this country from Europe and then later from many different countries and cultures. A "melting pot" it is often called. Most now believe that even the "Native Americans" immigrated here also by crossing a land (or ice) bridge from Asia to Alaska and downward to all of both North and South America – a process that would have taken many generations to accomplish.

Much later Europeans got in small, leaky sailing ships and spent months crossing the Atlantic, incurring loss of loved ones as they came. Even in our modern age people from Cuba and Viet Nam have boarded small boats to come to America. However it all occurred, one thing seems certain – it took initiative and grit to do it. It was more difficult than anything I can imagine and success was certainly not guaranteed. Many failed to make it; but, many did make it and started a new life.

In his book, *Mayflower,* Nathanial Philbrick[*] comments on what he believes became a unique marker for those early Americans that came to New England. He mentions two things that became characteristic. The first one had to do with the first Pilgrims and their effort to share everything, the work and all the provisions of the work. After the first year it quickly became apparent that some were doing most of the work while others very little – although they shared equally in the provisions. They quickly changed the approach to each family having their own property to establish their home plus a garden to grow food. The new way worked extremely well and became a foundation of one of the most important aspects of life for those early Americans, the right to property and the pursuit of happiness (which could be interpreted as all that sustains life…food and space to live your life as you wish it to be.)

The second thing Philbrick mentions is the reality that without the help of the Native American Indians who were already in New England and who had already learned how to hunt, grow food, and build shelter for the cold New England winters, the pilgrims would not have survived. In fact another group of immigrants from England came to Jamestown, Virginia and did not survive the first year, more came and struggled for some years before they figured out what was needed. But those who came to New England developed relationships with the Indians, out of necessity, and figured out more quickly how to adjust to this new world. That characteristic, Philbrick believes, has much to do with the rest of the story, the crossing and settling of America "from sea to shining sea".

I personally believe that these characteristics: the right to own property and pursue happiness along with the determination, grit, and willingness to learn new things and make adjustments as needed became a cornerstone for the culture that emerged to be so successful over the next 400 years.

Fast-forward 150 years to the founding of our country, The United States of America. **George Washington**, our first president, didn't even want the office. He felt his duty was to lead the army against the

---

[*] *The Mayflower, Nathaniel Philbrick, 2008 Putnam publishing*

British and then turn leadership over to someone else. After the events in New England, Bunker Hill, and New York the continental army moved south and found themselves in Valley Forge, along the banks of the Delaware river north of Philadelphia, at the onset of winter. It was a most difficult winter; the weather was extremely cold, provisions were low and difficult to find, and the troops didn't have the clothing necessary to stay warm and keep from freezing. General Washington had a warm home a day's ride away but he chose to stay with his troops. (It was normal for senior officers in those times to stay in their own home if it was not too distant.).

The British, on the other hand, wintered in Philadelphia, with plenty of provisions and warm sleeping quarters. As Washington and his army suffered, the British army enjoyed far better accommodations. At the end of the winter, Washington's continental army, their ranks depleted from the cold and lack of food and clothing, moved on the British. Emaciated as they were, they were also ready to fight and would follow this leader who was "with them", anywhere. They won battles they probably would have lost a year earlier and turned the tide of the war in their favor. They were the journeymen of our emerging nation, all of them. They were with Washington, the general over all the army, through thick and thin, to victory or defeat, no matter what...because he was "with them". There isn't an army in the world that can overcome the synergy and the momentum of an army so endowed!

It wasn't over yet, but it was the turning point and the rest is history as they say. But, we must take note of an important truth here – when men are challenged in the way war challenges men, the difference between winning and losing really does come down to two things: leaders who can be trusted to do the right thing, and soldiers who understand the objective and are willing to follow.

Another of our great leaders, **Abraham Lincoln,** split logs when he was young. His education was mostly self-taught. He had the "horse sense" that comes with all that and managed to lead the country embroiled in civil war back to unity. He didn't do it by edict or proclamation; he did it through collaboration with other leaders, some whom he didn't agree with. He knew he was better off engaging them than ignoring them. He also went to where the people were, to hear and assess first hand what they thought. It was not abnormal for Lincoln to just show up at an encampment of soldiers during the civil war just to listen to what they were thinking. When it became eminent that the South would soon surrender he conferred with General Grant, the leader of the Northern army. Together they created a plan to allow General Lee and the Southern army to surrender with dignity and respect and return to their homes with a horse and a rifle to begin the rebuilding process.

This may have been the only time in the history of war that the conquering side let the losers go home to rebuild without exacting heavy penalties (Heavy pillaging, burning property, rape…was typical for the conquering army in most wars in the world). The far sightedness of this as well as just the care and concern for his fellow man made Lincoln a leader for the ages – it reunited and began the restoration of our nation. Without his leadership it is hard to imagine what America would look like now!

There are many stories about this war period that show something of the American spirit and some of my favorites are the ones about Southern and Northern troops singing to each other songs popular in that time and if possible connecting face to face to talk. Even in the midst of war there was a sense of common heritage and common destiny.

The end of Slavery: A very key part of this century is the story of slavery, that part of American culture that started and functioned in a vastly different way than the rest. Black Africans were brought to America against their will and enslaved by white masters in the southern states. When America is described as a 'melting pot', I wonder to what extent African Americans are included; but the reality is they are as American as any of us irrespective of how they got here…we all come from immigrants, even the native American Indians. Certainly, they are owed respect and opportunity to become whatever they have in their hearts to become – the same as for those of us not African or black. I am pleased to see the tremendous improvement regarding this; but more has to happen and I trust it will. (See my article entitled Race in the addendum).

The Twentieth Century is proving to be a time of unparalleled growth economically on the positive side and world war on the negative side. As the world has moved more and more into a global marketplace, the quest for power on the part of "evil empires" has and is still occurring. This has always been true throughout history to some degree, typically contained to a region as opposed to being global.

In the early part of the century the growth of what became Adolph Hitler's Nazi regime, got its legs as a result of the world wide economic collapse and depression of 1929. He promised to correct the cause of the problems and got the ear of the German citizenry to the point of being able to take over the country and begin taking over countries that bordered. Hitler's real motivation, however, was *totalitarianism** – he wanted to achieve an obedient nation that met his personal vision: a pure race of people through eradication of any and all that didn't fit what he thought was pure. Six million Jews were a main focal point or this "cleansing". Through an alliance with Italy and Japan (the Axis powers) Hitler was well on his way to world domination.

In Europe the primary fighting ground was for France and the Benelux countries to the west and Poland and Russia to the east. Japan was after the Asian countries of China and Korea with Italy focused on the Mediterranean region. The opposing countries of England, France, and Russia (the Allies) were essentially losing the war and it seemed very possible that the Axis powers would succeed.

It was then that the United States of America got involved. They had played a supportive role of providing supplies and weapons but were

---

* *Totalitarianism is a political system in which the state – central government – holds total control over the society and seeks to control all aspects of public and private life wherever possible. Prime examples are: Nazi Germany, The Soviet Union, and North Korea*

trying to avoid a "boots on the ground" fight if possible. As it became clear that more would be needed to thwart Hitler, much more…The US entered the fight. By this time the German army was controlling Europe, pushing their way to Moscow, and along with Italy had control of the Mediterranean access points to Europe. It would take an unbelievable effort to overcome what the Axis powers had achieved.

The action taken is the theme of the movie **The Longest Day – D-day, the battle of Normandy…**it was the beginning of the end for the Nazi evil empire. Essentially it was a huge plan to land the Allied armies (essentially the British, Canadian and American Armies) in Europe through the beaches of Normandy on the French coast. The action took weeks to plan and prepare for what was hoped to be a one-day event where thousands of Allied troops and equipment would be landed and moved inland. To accomplish the feat several hundred ships were "scuttled" – sunk in the incoming surf just beyond the beaches to form a reef. The landing craft with troops and equipment could then move up to the beaches in the quieter water, inside the man made reef and off load their cargos.

Of course they met resistance, incredible resistance from the Germans who were well "dug in" in positions to see the beaches clearly…the Allied troops were sitting ducks as they came ashore; but they came and they kept coming, even as they saw their buddies shot down they came. This took place June 6, 1944 and was the beginning of an all out assault to bring Adolph Hitler and his armies to a halt. There are different estimates but about 10,000 men were casualties and 2000 aircraft were lost just in the battle for Normandy. It took another year but in September of 1945 the Allies were finally victorious, The German army was defeated and Adolph Hitler was dead from suicide.

(*Something re results for the war in the Pacific*)

The resulting toll for World War 2 was 85 million people, killed, wounded, or missing – both military and civilian included. The number itself is astounding, but the toll in other ways may have been even more astounding, For example, following the war the Soviet Union began yet another effort to begin an attempt to take over the world…an emergence of a second "evil empire" in a period of less than 50 years.

This was called the **Cold War,** because the effort was more political and threat based than all out declaration of war. Results were similar, however, in terms of nations being taken over by what was now known as the Soviet Union. All of what had been Eastern Europe was soon under the control of the Soviets, actually a result of agreements made by the allied leadership of Chamberlin, Stalin and Roosevelt. As it became clear that the tide had changed in World War 2, they divided the spoils, so to speak. Each Nation; Russia, Great Britain and the US, were to take responsibility for the restoration of a portion of the European nations conquered and now freed from the Axis empire.

The countries designated to be in Russian control took a different turn very quickly as the Soviets applied their own brand of totalitarianism. That was Hitler's objective and now it was apparent that the Russia (the Soviet Union) had a similar objective. Joseph Stalin, who took over the country in 1922, had a similar approach as Hitler… he executed anyone who not in alignment with the goals of the state, but his end goal was not the same; Hitler was going for a "pure race" of Arian people, the Soviets were pushing more of a political agenda – communism, which sounds better to begin with until one realizes that at the core are a few who control it all and the masses suffer.

Like the totalitarianism of Hitler this new totalitarianism had to be stopped before it went too far. The problem was how; it wasn't the kind of situation where one nation out fights another. No, this was political, and it was more a question of who would outwit the other. It was a show of power on each side – each had nuclear power and that had to be dealt with carefully. If one chose to use it they must be prepared to receive it. So far, as of this writing, no one has been willing to take that chance after what became quite obvious from the Nagasaki and Hiroshima bombings to end the Japanese effort in World War Two.

After 30 years or so of posturing it became clear to the Soviets that what they were trying to achieve wasn't working. Their satellite countries in Eastern Europe were constantly a problem and the Western Europe Alliance along with the leadership of the US were proving difficult to maneuver around. In the summer of 1987 president Ronald Reagan gave a speech in front of the Brandenburg gate of the Berlin wall in Germany – a wall built by the Soviet Communist Regime to fully separate Western Europe and the US from the Soviet Union satellite countries.

That afternoon, Reagan said:

> *We welcome change and openness; for we believe that freedom and security go together, that the advance of human liberty can only strengthen the cause of world peace. There is one sign the Soviets can make that would be unmistakable, that would advance dramatically the cause of freedom and peace. General Secretary Gorbachev, if you seek peace, if you seek prosperity for the Soviet Union and Eastern Europe, if you seek liberalization, come here to this gate. Mr. Gorbachev, open this gate.* **Mr. Gorbachev, tear down this wall!** *(Ronald Reagan, address at the Brandenburg Gate, June 12, 1987).*

The wall, built in 1961, was demolished in 1989 – two years after Reagan's speech. No one would say that Reagan defeated the Soviet Union, most would say that it collapsed under it's own weight; but most, would agree that Reagan's persistence and aggressive posture against the Soviet Agenda sped up the process.

I confess, I like Ronald Reagan; in fact I admire him greatly. He was pretty good in a wide variety of things, smart but not brilliant, not the best politician ever, but pretty good!

So why do I like him? I like him because he knew these things about himself and it didn't stop him. In fact, I think it pushed him to reach out to others in ways that many (can I say most) leaders never do. He communicated well but he also listened well, and incorporated what he heard into who he was, how he thought, and how he acted. He was a lot like Washington and Lincoln, especially in the way of not assuming he had all the answers.

Also, He had history on his side, American history, especially in terms of what America had become as a world power and the way that was used to defeat the threat of world domination by Adolph Hitler and his evil empire. Certainly, a huge part of what Reagan and America had to offer was Americans, millions of them by this time, and a work ethic that was embraced by all. The work ethic that says, if it's worth doing it's worth doing well and that means we don't stop until we're finished. That's what happened at Normandy that long day in 1944. It's what Americans have done since they first arrived on this continent.

So, as Ronald Reagan emerged as a leader of a state and then the country, he was one of those people, a journeyman if you will! I believe that when he said, Mr. *Gorbachev, tear down that wall*, it was way more than just him saying it – he was the microphone to be sure but he spoke with the full weight of America behind him, what it had become and what it could do.

How else do you explain the events that followed a couple of years later, as Soviet States (Poland, Czechoslovakia, Hungary, Romania, Yugoslavia, etc.) refused to bow their knee to Russia any longer? Those states also understood what Reagan had backing him up and they trusted that America would be there for them just as it was for Western Europe a few short years earlier. Reagan may have been average in a lot of things but he knew who he was, he knew the American people's resolve to correct injustice in the world, and he trusted the God he followed to lead the way.

So, for a number of years, the Russian conquest has been stalled, but as we now know, not stopped. It still lurks! And of course there seems to be another developing "evil empire" aiming to create their own totalitarian regime and domination at least of the western world as we know it. Yes, I'm speaking of the Arab world in the Middle East – at least part of it, however you slice and dice that question. We've gone from Hitler's quest to purify the world population by getting rid of all that don't fit the mold – the Nazi mold – to the Russian quest to control the world population by making it one big commune with all the power at the top in the hands of a privileged few – to now another effort to purify the world population by making all conform to a religious standard or be eliminated (not too much different from Adolph Hitler's or Joseph Stalin's quests).

At this stage the conflict in the Middle East is more than a "cold war", and although it's not yet WWIII, it has moved beyond a conflict. There have been plenty of battles and lives lost on both sides; in fact, it is most difficult to tell just where the lines are drawn for the enemy we face because if they aren't killing westerners they are killing others in the middle east that you would think they would have some affinity for. Not so, this is a religious war (irrespective of what some think) and they, the enemy that goes by many names, will kill any who don't agree with them, including those seemingly of their own race.

Whatever the origins and ethos of the current enemy they are our enemy and they threaten our being as much as earlier ones, if not more; and so far we don't seem to have the resolve to challenge it and correct it that we had as recently as 30 years ago. I'm not laying this at the feet of normal citizens, I lay it at the feet of our leaders. I won't try to assess the reasons for this, although I do have some ideas, as I'm sure anyone reading this would. What I will say is "it's not there"; the leadership we have seen over our history from those who first came to this country to George Washington to Abraham Lincoln to Ronald Reagan is simply not there today. We do need to get it back!!

CHAPTER 6

ECONOMIC DEVELOPMENT

The role of freedom and personal initiative in the building of our nation was in play from the beginning of the formation of "America". It can be seen from the earliest efforts of those who emigrated here and later as the children and grandchildren of those first Americans moved west.

I can only imagine what it was like for a family to move from another continent to America. My own family moved from Germany to the Catskill Mountains in upstate New York In the 1850's and homesteaded a farm on one of those mountains. Other families came to the East coast and then made the journey to the west coast – in a wagon pulled by oxen – to homestead in a variety of places ranging from mountains to plains to coastal areas. Still others wound up in the major cities of the time – New York, Boston, San Francisco, Chicago, and Los Angeles. Much of the country would remain virtually untouched for many more years but as the population grew – these were eventually reached and settled as well. By 1800 the population was 5 million people, by 1900 it had grown to 76 million, and today it's over 300 million.

How did they survive? There were no government programs, no houses to move into, no jobs and, for the most part, no ready food supply. The food that did exist naturally was not enough for the population growth that occurred.

They survived because they took the skills and capabilities they had, to clear land, build houses and plant fields, and then build everything else they had a need for, from wagons and wagon wheels to furniture and kitchen utensils. They each couldn't make everything they needed so they developed a system of trading which allowed each to eventually obtain everything they needed. The result was little businesses, attached to the family home. These little businesses produced things ranging from tools for farming to utensils for cooking and caring for a house. Most had a barn of some sort to house animals, and a field or two to grow vegetables and perhaps some grape vines or apple trees. All of this became known as "cottage industry" and it was the economic engine for the first 250 years of America's history.

As the emerging generations and cottage industry developed there was a personal development approach that worked quite well. It was a system where a young person would *apprentice* to an older, experienced person – like a son or daughter to a father or mother, or to a teacher, a business owner, a pastor… The word apprenticeship means *a system of training (developing) a new generation.* This became a fairly well organized system to develop a whole variety of skills and capabilities: construction craft skills like wood working, iron work, plumbing, electrical wiring; household skills like cooking, sewing/making clothing, decorating; and business skills like selling, accounting, planning, organizing, and supervising. Actually, this approach was already in practice in many other parts of the world to some degree, and many who immigrated brought skills with them to pass on to next generations.

The Cottage Age eventually ushered in **The Industrial Age** in the 1800's. That development was created by the discovery/invention of steam power systems and electricity which enabled machines to be created to do what was being done by hand or hand operated machines – the result was bigger and faster machines, which yielded more product and in many situations lowered the cost of something that had been produced by hand labor and one at a time. The same sort of apprenticeship approach was useful during that period as well although the seeds of dismantlement were sown as companies grew ever larger and the task of preparing workers became more like "sheep dipping" than the development of each single individual to become what he/she hoped for and was capable of.

Another result was a change in how leadership worked. In the Cottage Age it was Mom and Dad who typically managed and led the organization to do whatever it was tasked to do. As these enterprises grew there was a movement toward professional managers, trained to lead an organization that was getting bigger and bigger.

It simply wasn't possible for these managers to concentrate on the development of each person, therefore training became focused on groups and also focused on only one or two things that the individuals would do. It resulted in organizations that were like boxes (boundaries) that defined each person's responsibility. These boxes were part of a bigger box, which, in turn was part of an even bigger box. The professionally trained leaders were called managers (this word was seldom used in the Cottage age). They were trained to manage and control people, not to lead and develop individuals.

Just as the business world has experienced the addition of professional managers who often manage and control more than they lead and develop, we have seen our government leadership at all levels move in a corresponding way to professional politicians who are controlling the agendas of the country, states and communities, often with little input from those they are governing. In the early days of the American story the people that led were also journeymen – they did it in addition to tilling their fields and bringing in a crop.

Our society and economy began as craft/skill based oriented – each person knew how to make something and some started businesses or became a key part of an organization as a small group supervisor. These were the "Journeymen" of the time and as the large organizations emerged, it wasn't unusual to see Journeymen providing the needed leadership between senior management and the workers. This approach has been around since the Roman Empire...in our own military; a sizable army unit can be effectively led by non commissioned officers (sergeants, master sergeants and chief master sergeants). In sports it has long been understood that without the journeymen (those who have been there for a while: position players, as well as the celebrity players - even more so in many cases) a team couldn't function much less win a championship.

In recent years our culture has moved away from the Industrial Age; much has been exported to other countries – China for example, who now does the manufacturing and send us the completed product. We are now clearly in a new age; the **information age**, a combination of large and small organizations. In fact today there are over 20 million 'companies of one' (single owner companies) in the US – not exactly a return to the cottage age but certainly some resemblance to that era. For the larger "tech companies", the work force is now known as 'knowledge workers', with the work focused on creating software to run the array of websites, data bases, etc. for the millions of computers that are now the basis of nearly everything, from automobiles to airplanes to movies to…well, you name it. It is an amazing new world and not without it's issues. From a work culture perspective the "knowledge workers" are less involved in anything beyond their corner of that world. Many are contract workers moving from gig to gig… and now more and more of the work is being contracted to other counties.

Another emerging reality of the emerging generation is that they are not interested in working for someone else. They want to do their own thing, like start their own business or sub contract themselves to larger companies. No doubt, many of these young people are developing as the journeymen and journeywomen of today; but it remains to be seen just how it all plays out for the future.

The leaders (journeymen and journeywomen) of the last several hundred years of our history seemed always to have the national interest in mind. It is not clear how the combination of our "celebrity leadership culture" along with the "contractor mentality" of our emerging generations will develop as we move into the future. If we continue the way we are going it is quite possible that the future leadership potential of our nation will be reduced and possibly reduced significantly.

Journeymen and journeywomen are the backbone of any organization – be it a small team, a huge army., or a nation. As such they are the backbone of a culture and only time will tell whether the effectiveness of that layer of our society's leadership will remain strong or simply become nonexistent. If it is the latter then we will be reduced to no more than any other weak nation.

CHAPTER 7

THE SOCIALIZATION OF AMERICA

"There are more Americans on welfare than in the work force!" This quote is from an article by Tom Jeffrey in TownHall.com on January 21, 2013. He compares the 35.4 percent number of 109,631,000 Americans getting welfare payments reported by the Census Bureau for 2013 with 105,862,000 full time workers reported for the same year. The premise made by Jeffrey is debated due to some welfare recipients also being in the work force, but the point is clear. We have become a nation dependent on the central government more than has ever been the case.

When the Great Depression began in 1929 there were about 18 million elderly, disabled, and single mothers with children living at a bare subsistence level in the US, about 15 % of the population. By 1933 another 13 million had lost jobs and were added to the number that needed help, increasing the size of this group to 24% of the total population. In 1935, a national welfare system was established for the first time (the Social Security Act). Up to that point individual States had been the primary source of help. As we all know President Roosevelt spearheaded this effort, which began with an effort to create jobs but soon included more – unemployment and old age insurance, benefits for poor single mothers and their children along with other dependent persons, etc.

It is interesting to note that, although Roosevelt sponsored this Act, he also had reservations: *"The lessons of history, confirmed by the evidence immediately before me, show conclusively that continued dependence upon relief induces a spiritual and moral disintegration fundamentally destructive to the national fiber. To dole out relief in this way is to administer a narcotic, a subtle destroyer of the human spirit. (Franklin D. Roosevelt, State of the Union Address 1935; underline mine).*

When I contrast the number of Americans that are dependent on the central government relative to where we started as a country, it's pretty clear that our culture has changed from "can do" to "can't do", at least for a large portion of the population. I suspect that for all of the population there is less in terms of rugged individualism and self-actualization today, especially relative to those early Americans. To some degree all of us are dependent on the government; think taxes, health care and now marriage. Even free speech has now become cloudy in terms of what is appropriate and what isn't. I wonder if the word Totalitarianism is beginning to fit for America.

When Roosevelt and our government enacted the Social Security Act in 1935, I doubt they knew what they had unleashed, although based on Roosevelt's quote above he did have an idea. I can understand that something had to be done and I can understand that there will always be poor or disabled people amongst us who cannot care for themselves. I believe it is a duty of those of us who are not poor or disabled to give assistance in some way. I further believe that left alone, the typical American will, and does, come to the aid of those less fortunate. But when the central government does it, and does it poorly most of the time, it becomes something expected as if it is a right.

If it is necessary to provide oversight in some way, to assure fairness, etc., then let that be a responsibility of the states, and communities within the states, not the federal government. That is the way it was before 1935, and although there are those that would argue that it didn't work well, it did work. I think the numbers vouch for that; 15% of the population before 1930 and 35% now, and that is just welfare. When the other socialization aspects are added; taxes, health care, marriage and family, speech, etc. we are all affected in ways that our predecessors were not.

It's impossible to calculate the net effect all of this has on our culture; but to say it hasn't affected it is ludicrous! I've been in enough organizational situations to know that moral is highly dependent on the level of influence a person has for their own life and when you take much of that away through rules and procedures determined by a small, central leadership group, the productivity can be measured to be only half of what a fully functioning organization* can deliver. I believe we are there in America regarding productivity.

The Family Unit has been an extremely important institution throughout the history of America – it was in the very beginning, it still is but is most definitely losing ground. A primary indicator of this is the rate of marriage divorces, because that event for most families is a major game changer and not for the better in most cases. The statistic has moved from a 3% divorce rate in 1870 to 50% by 1980 *(National Center for Health Statistics)*. What is interesting to note in this data is that there is a pronounced uptick beginning in 1965 when the divorce rate was 27%. It increased over the next 10 years to 48% and then 50% in 1980 where it has hovered to this point. This is almost a doubling, which seems unbelievable. So the question of course is why and what does that have to do with us today in 2016?

This period of divorce increase translates into more dysfunctional families, families of only one parent, families with no father (much more than with no mother); this, in turn, translates into children raised in day care centers, etc. without the family development of the primary values and characteristics for a successful life. Of course all of this moves to the next generations and for some families…they never dig out of the hole…so sad, and so preventable if the original divorce that sponsored it all was avoided. In an earlier time it was, more often than not - the husband and the wife "stuck it out" and "worked it out", often

---

* *An organization in which each individual plays a key role.*

with their children being hardly aware of what was happening; or if they did the Mom and Dad had the sense to explain it all in a way that was loving and considerate of each other and certainly of their children. The children of these families, both the dysfunctional and traditional (Mom, dad and children), in turn will typically produce families of similar qualities.

Dysfunction and poverty: An aspect of our nation that most of us find deeply troubling is the great dysfunction amongst those of the younger generations. On one hand, some of them represent perhaps the brightest and most capable generation ever – looking forward to making their way in the world and not looking for a handout but expecting to work for it. These will surely become our future leaders. But, on the other hand, there are far too many that are someplace between struggling and outright failing – at life. This should be no surprise but it always makes me sad when I think about it.

It should be no surprise, when you put together the family dysfunction in our country, especially the missing fathers, with the factors of poverty, poor schools, poor role models, leaders who inflame rather than lead... well, what can you expect. The poverty statistic for families without a father is 30% versus 5.8% for a two-parent family. We still have ghettos near or in our cities that are worse than anything in the so called "Third World"...so bad that police forces avoid them as much as possible (no wonder really, the danger of being hauled in to jail for enforcing the law is sometimes as bad as being shot out right).

All of this ultimately results in serious levels of crime ranging from theft to murder and rape and everything in between. And then there are the riots, and the gangs – this is America? Again, we shouldn't be surprised, the perfect storm is occurring as three storm fronts come together; breakdown of the family...poverty...leaders who enflame!

What if we reverse that? How about leaders who lead...a creation of systems and approaches to teach and sponsor enterprise and job development to eradicate poverty, and education of young men and women to focus on and develop families who become what they were when America began…loving, functional, and generational. It will take a generation to recover this but it is recoverable, and it is certainly worthwhile!

Wars and Social Revolution: The 1960's was a time that is now known as the "60's social revolution", a time of "becoming free" for the generation of young people at the time. It was a time of experimentation with things before considered to be taboo – drugs, sex, music, dress, schooling, and politics being at the top of the list.

At the same time the country was into an unpopular war in Viet Nam that turned out to be unwinnable. Soldiers came home to unwelcoming crowds that were unappreciative of their efforts – they were called names, spit at and rejected. When you compare this to the earlier wars of the 20th century – in which the soldiers were admired and very appreciated for their service and the loss or crippling of life for so many men, it's hard to imagine the damage done to the Viet Nam Vets - we really cannot appreciate what that did to that generation of young men.

Further, when you connect the effects of "The Sixties" social revolution with the effects of this war… what is the total result? We know that the divorce rate nearly doubled between 1965 and 1975, and we know that to this day men of that war and the war in the middle east – another unpopular war that cannot be won it seems – suffer from PTSD which is a game changer for most of them in the wrong direction. It is no wonder divorces have increased and the traditional family has been impacted negatively.

Then, to top it all off, the Social Security Act, which should help all of this, in many ways just adds to the feeling of inadequacy and hopelessness instead of the 'can do' attitude of Americans for the past 400 years. There are likely many who say, thank God for these government programs; but for others of us, it's like an unseen force bringing a seemingly good thing to the people, which in the long run will weaken a large portion of the American culture. (FDR quote in beginning of chapter)

Where are the Men? It seems very clear to me that the role of men through this 400-year period was instrumental to the success of America. It is also clear that the role of women was likewise instrumental. I see no difference in the value of those contributions; without each, none of what became the American culture would have happened. America would have remained a continent of land and animals.

At the end of the second chapter I indicated concern about men, that it seemed like they, as a group, had lost something in the way of their collective zeal for life; not true of all I said, but true of many – perhaps even the majority. As I think about men as Journeymen – I see that diminishing as well. It's as if men have lost their "center of gravity" and don't know up from down!

As I was researching material for this book I ran across an Article by Binyamin Appelbaum, New York Times, Dec. 11, 2014, called *The Vanishing Male Worker: How America fell behind.* I have included that article in its entirety in the addendum. Essentially Mr. Appelbaum expresses the fact that, *"The share of prime-age men – those 25-54 years old – who are not working has more than tripled since the late 1960's to 16%"*

He provides further information from a New York Times/CBS News/Kaiser Family Poll about the group of 30 million prime age Americans without jobs (10 million of which are men):

- *Deep changes in American society have made it easier for them to live without working. These changes include the availability of federal disability benefits, the decline of marriage – which means fewer men to provide for children, and the rise of the Internet, which has reduced the isolation of unemployment.*
- *It has become harder for men to find higher paying jobs.* (My note: High paying manufacturing jobs from the Industrial era have largely left the country, or been shut down)

- *A smaller work force is likely to lead to a slower growing economy.*
- *In follow up interviews men described days spent mostly at home, chewing up dwindling resources, relying on friends, strangers and the federal government…30% had used food stamps while 33% said they had taken food from a nonprofit or religious group.*

Mr Appelbaum further quotes from the American Enterprise Institute and the Institute for Family Studies that, *37 percent of the decline in male employment since 1979 could be explained by their retreat from marriage and fatherhood.*

Mr. Appelbaum summarizes his research this way:

The decline of work (for men) is divisible into three related trends:

1. *Young men are spending more years in school, delaying their entry into the workforce but potentially improving their eventual economic prospects.*
2. *At the other end of the 25-54 year spectrum, many older men who lost jobs have fallen back on disability benefits or started to draw on retirement savings. For some of those men who worked in manufacturing or construction, and now can only find service work, the obstacle is not just the difference in pay; it is also <u>the humiliation of being on public display</u>* (underline mine).
3. *In the third group are men…too young to retire but often ill equipped to find new work.* He quotes an out of work electrician who says, *"I lost my sense of worth, you know what I mean?"* When asked what he does he says, *"…I say nothing. I'm not an electrician anymore"*

Mr Appelbaum has put his finger on my concern. Men are not adjusting well to the new economy and the new cultural norms, which feel to them as if their role – in the family, the workplace, and society in general - has been at least reduced, and in some cases…eliminated! They are finding it difficult to journey through this new world. Certainly it's a mixed bag and while some are doing very well, my guess is that <u>many</u> more are not.

To repeat a statement I made at the end of Chapter two: "It's not that they've given up totally; but they have reconciled themselves to the reality they find themselves in and "going along with it", meaning not "rocking the boat", but not really giving their best either. That is not how men used to be. Up to and including WWII men were ready to do whatever they were called to do"

Actually I believe this didn't begin to occur until about the 1970's, with the culmination of a war that couldn't be won (Viet Nam), the 60's social revolution, the beginning of the removal of God in public schools, and the doubling of the divorce statistics, Major industries were beginning to downsize by the 80's, along with the advent of the Information age. By 2000 both Information Age companies and what was left of the Industrial Age companies were outsourcing jobs and production to other countries. It seems to me that throughout that period men began to be affected adversely and the "vanishing' began!

Technology: a blessing or a curse? Smart phones, the internet, on line shopping from the comfort of your home, a job from the comfort of your home, Google to provide instant answers; what a blessing…or is it? In light of the previous section, "Where are the Men", I wonder if technology is also a contributor? In the article re *The Vanishing Male Worker* is this observation:

> …*Technology has made unemployment less lonely. Tyler Cowen, an economist at George Mason University, argues that the Internet allows men to entertain themselves and find friends at a much lower cost than did previous generations.*

I have no doubt that this is true and I would expand the concept to women and children. When was the last time you saw kids just playing outside, being imaginative and creating games, or building a fort. And how about the exporting of jobs to other countries – that is largely in the technical sector or through the use of technology of the market place. Most companies have exported work to other countries where there are people skilled enough to do it and who will accept much lower pay.

With technology a person in India or the Philippines can take your call and if he or she speaks American English (yes, I know, most don't but they are improving) you can't tell if they are in the US or on the other side of the world.

So, back to the question, is technology a blessing or a curse? I guess I would say it can be either, on one hand it can really make life easier and more productive in the sense of our own personal accomplishments; but, I wonder if it could isolate some so much that they are really no more than a pinhead of data to the world around them, no one knows them and no one cares. If they are sick and die there is no one to bury them. Sounds awful I know, but think about it…is it possible if we let some things continue too long in the wrong direction?

God Bless America: Presidents have finished their State of the Union address with this statement forever as far as I know. **God Protect us** was a plea uttered many times by those first boatloads of people coming to American in the early 1600's; that was all they could hope for half way across the Atlantic ocean in a crowded sailing ship where most of the passengers were sea sick. To some extent that is the way it has been for the better part of 400 years, we need God's protection and we need his blessing. I grew up in farm country and I have never met a farmer who didn't have at least some measure of faith in almighty God to come through for him in terms of weather, health of family and animals, crop success, etc.

Our early leaders were men and women of faith, it can be seen in our founding documents, The Constitution, Declaration of Independence and The Bill of Rights:

> *The Bill of Rights reflects the Christian heritage of our nation. The idea of human dignity, that we are created in the image of God, forms the theological basis for human equality and our core principle of liberty (Genesis 1:27, Leviticus 25:10, Matthew 25:40, Mark 12:31). The fundamental basis of religious freedom in human nature secures our rights and limits government. There*

*is a higher authority than civil authority, the laws of God (Acts 5:29). The Declaration of Independence recognizes God, the Creator, that there is a Supreme Judge - Divine Providence, from whom we receive certain inalienable rights, that of Life, Liberty, and the Pursuit of Happiness. The moral teachings of the **Bible** establish the common standards of right and wrong required in ourselves and in government to guide private and public life. The rights and responsibilities of citizenship are learned in the primary institutions of civil society - the family, church, and the community - to teach virtue, shape character, and form productive and upright individuals.* (biblescripture.net)

From those early years to the mid 50's when I grew up, faith, the Christian faith, though practiced in many different ways, was an important element to Americans. And then that faith began to be challenged. In the 50's when I was a young lad it was very normal to pray and read Bible stories in school. It was as much a part of everyday life as standing to pledge allegiance to the flag. It was also normal to be challenged as a young lad to work hard, to respect my elders, and to respect the young ladies of the opposite sex. School was as much about character building – American character building – as it was about Reading, wRiting, aRithmatic, the "three R's" as they were called.

I remember an incident in which I was caught throwing a "spit ball" at another student just as the teacher walked in the door. I was in the seventh grade. The teacher picked me up by my shirt collar and sent me to the principle's office to be "talked to". That was easy, it could have been a whipping but the offense wasn't <u>all</u> that bad in the mind of the principle. So, I got a lecture and went home at the end of the day as normal. I had noticed a small tear in my shirt where the teacher had grabbed me and I thought to myself, "Wow, will my mother be mad at my teacher!"

Didn't turn out the way I thought it would. I showed the tear to my mother and told her who did it. She didn't even ask what I did to provoke such a thing. Her response was, "well you probably deserved it and you better not do whatever you were doing again! I hope you have learned a lesson." Can you imagine the furor that would be made today about that teacher, at a minimum he would lose his job! Not in those days. In a small town parents knew the teachers (they made a point to) and they trusted them to do the right thing, That teacher never even knew he had torn my shirt because I didn't tell him and my parents didn't go raise a fuss. It was my lesson to be learned –no one else, and here I am about 60 years later telling you about it…It registered and it was part of my education.

Sometimes we think of God as an entity, or a concept perhaps, but as I have grown older I see him as a person – Jesus, the son of God is who I picture as God, and there are character traits that go along with that person which is well described in the New Testament Bible. That is what our country has been about for 400 years and that is what we're beginning to lose in my estimation, and in the estimation of many I'm sure.

Most biblically based historians point to 1963 and 1973 as the years when God was significantly pushed away, particularly in the public schools. 1963 is the year when prayer and the reading of the Bible in public schools were outlawed and 1973 the year killing of unborn children was legalized. Since that time it is estimated that 50 million children have been killed. Today, it is more evident than ever that life begins at conception so my use of the word killing is appropriate - it is a life created by God …*in his image!!*

Digress to tell Azeriah story???

It would seem, certainly, that we have regressed as a Nation from what our founders envisioned, at least in terms of our embracing the "Godly principles" that originally guided those founders and which, in reality, were inherent to our rise to the world power. The question one must ask is. "Has it all gone to our heads, have we come to believe we did it, not God?" If so we must consider another set of "three R's"…Repent, Reconcile and Restore:

➢ Repent: turn from the way we are going, to the direction we originally started from.

➢ Reconcile: ask our creator God, the God who made us each "in his own Image" to forgive us for our selfish acts and attitudes

➢ Restore: Fix and rebuild what has been torn down…essentially the place of God in our lives both private and public

CHAPTER 8

THE BOTTOM LINE

In the centuries that have passed since the pilgrims landed there are some distinct and unmistakable themes. The first one is the *quest for freedom:* freedom from narrow religiosity, from autocratic government, from poverty; and right along with freedom, *the desire to see what's on the other side*...the other side of the ocean, the other side of the mountains, etc. I believe those two themes say it all! These were the themes that caused America to become America in the very beginning - *the land of the free*, characterized by rugged, self-reliant individuals who also could "team up" with others to make something work.

You can see it as the pilgrims came in the 1600's, you can see it as the westward migration took place in the 1700's, you can see it in the fight for independence in the latter 1700's, you can see it in the struggle to end slavery and re-unite the country following the civil war, and you can see it as we faced the scourges from Hitler's evil empire and the Soviet Union communist attempts to conquer the world in the 1900's. It is unmistakable in the formation of our Nation and also unmistakable in the hearts of men and women – the desire to be free and plot your own course is what makes America...beautiful.

In recent years America has led in most important areas; Education, technical achievements, military prowess, business growth, government style, etc. The leaders come and go, and certainly some leave their mark – some good and some not so good. But it is journeymen and woman that really makes it all possible. Ask a very talented NFL quarterback about that, or ask a "Level five" business leader (see *Good to Great* by Jim Collins), or ask a US president who isn't so full of himself that he has no idea. Ask a Pastor of a large church, or ask the principle/president of a good school or college.

New themes began to emerge as we left the 1800's and entered the 1900's. The beginning of large organizational thinking – both in terms of business and government; the industrial revolution turned everything on it's head, small became large and the individual began to lose his way...now he was a number rather than an individual; and, when the depression of 1939 occurred, many weren't even a number – they lost all they had.

Along came the government to fix things and that did get the country moving but it also set in motion something from which we have not yet recovered – dependency. The self reliant, highly capable, individual American was now just an irrelevant number in a big organized system (actually pretty disorganized), unable to really care for him or herself.

Other themes emerged; the sixties brought new thinking into our culture that was more negative than positive, a "social revolution" that hurt people in the long run rather than help them. That, along with the effects of wars that could not be won, higher and higher taxation - paid by a few to support the many who were now dependent on the government; all of this has seriously damaged many in our population, some to the point of simply "vanishing" (see chapter 7).

Oh there are those who have done well, which has added to a growing gap between the "haves" and "have-nots". Another theme is the movement of vast parts of our population from rural settings to cities and large metropolitan areas. The inevitability of slum areas in most of these large metropolitan areas was virtually assured, adding to the feeling of being a "have not" if you lived in one – and isolated now in big city without the "where-with-all" to even see the American dream much less move toward it.

The growing reality is that America is growing in Silos – a word that is meant for big vertical cylinders that hold grain, but now also used to describe an organizational phenomenon, which occurs as various units see themselves differently and are not willing to spend any time trying to find common vision and principles. America, it appears, has grown into Silos. People group silos for example – what used to be termed a "melting pot" has seemingly become – or becoming – a series of cultural silos, some quite big and others small but growing. Another grouping of silos can be noticed regarding life styles such as religions or an array of other life styles.

But the silos that are most noticeable are Political, and there are two primary ones – Democrats or Republicans. All of the other silos are claimed by one or the other of these as constituencies and the lack of much agreement between the many leads to a kind of paralysis at the National level which is supposed to provide leadership for the country along with the President and his staff, which has turned into a silo of its own it seems! All of this is where the professional politicians do their thing, the idea of citizen representation little more than a token of what it was meant to be when the founding fathers originally developed our constitution and physical government structure.

The American Dream, which began in 1620, produced the most powerful nation in the world 325 years later, at the conclusion of WWII. This is a distinction that has lasted only 70 years. The culture we have understood to be distinctly 'American' has been eroded largely as a result of many decisions made by the country's leaders over that 70 year period – decisions that have led to not winning wars, social give away programs that greatly exceed anything FDR envisioned*...also killing babies, destruction of the American family unit, movement by industry to other countries, advent of the information age which seems to promote a narrower kind of individual.

To Summarize:

The *Character* of our country has moved from rugged, self reliant individuals who desire to be free to a culture of organizational silos – each different, each pursuing different objectives, if pursuing anything at all. The result is no progress and an overall feeling of being stuck with no room to move.

Our *Leadership,* used to be an "up from the ranks" approach - Journeymen and women taking responsibility wherever they were with some being drawn up to senior roles of leadership: for governing the country, managing a businesses, guiding our educational institutions, and anything else needed in a given community. Much of this has become professionalized with each leader (elected or appointed) following their own ideas and agendas and very little connection with the citizenry of the country – a primary principle in the beginning and one that functioned well until recently.

The **Economic and Social Development** aspects of our culture were once woven together through an entrepreneurial, free enterprise, family based system, which functioned by a clear appreciation of the principles found in the Judeo/Christian Bible – and expressed in the counties founding documents. These aspects worked also worked well through the beginning of the 20th century and began to erode in the second half as clarified earlier.

---

* FDR said, *"Continued dependence upon relief induces a spiritual and moral disintegration (which is) fundamentally destructive to the national fiber. To dole out relief in this way is to administer a narcotic, a subtle destroyer of the human spirit."* His intention was that this relief would be temporary and, of course, that has not been the case, indeed, it has been amplified and, indeed, Roosevelt's description of the results is accurate!

Now, the culture is growing more and more dependent on social systems along with a "contractor" mentality for workers, who are unable to view any job as a "career". They are considered expendable and quickly released when the work changes and different skills needed. There is a growing strong desire to return to systems where there is more loyalty in both directions – that allow career oriented work systems, which compliment business success. (There are several good examples today where this is true with both objectives being accomplished)

The contrast of this with the first 400 years of America's existence is that the strong patriotic view of most Americans, that caused the Nation to become strong, and in fact - <u>The</u> World Power - that view is fading! Add to that the feeling on the part of many individual Americans that the American Dream is no longer attainable provides an explanation for the question by some, "What has happened to our country?" Or the lament from others, "we have lost our way!"

<u>Timeline of American Progress</u>

	Character	Leadership	Economic/ Social Dev
1600's	*Rugged Indiv* *Self reliance* *Desire to be free*	*Up from the ranks* *Journeymen and women* *As needed by community*	*Family/Cottage based* *Entrepreneurial, free* *enterprise*
1700's	*Nationalistic* *Desire to be free as a country*	*Up from the ranks* *Beginning of National Leaders, National vision*	*Same as above*
1800's	*Divided,* *civil war* *Slavery ended* *Country reunited*	*Representative leadership,* *State and Federal, still up from the ranks*	*Industrial Revolution: Large organizations Jobs versus skills*

1900's	*Rural to city* *Loss of individual* *Identity, War* *Big Business*	*Professional managers* *and politicians – less* *connection to the people* *Strong Ldrs –* *World pwr*	*Great depression* *Creation National* *Social Security System* *60's social revolution*
2000's	*Cultural silo-ing* *People group* *focus replacing* *National pride*	*Loss of Resolve to fight* *More political, less* *vision* *Less representative of* *the people*	*Growing dependence* *on social services;* *Tech growth/job loss* *Desire to go back*

Bottom Line

2017	*Culturally silo'd* *No progress,* *sense of* *Stalemate - Stuck* *Loss of National* *pride*	*Lack of Vision* *High dependency on* *central gov't, Prof Ldrs* *Less representation* *of the people*	*Strong desire to return* *to values of Freedom –* *giving up, Contractor* *mentality*

Add to this the reality that we've become an Urban Culture (80% 0f the US population lives in an urban environment). This means several things: it means that there are fewer small town communities with the relationships that used to dot the country 50 to 70 years ago, it means that many live in crowded circumstances with little potential to make a difference. It means that most people toil in jobs they really don't like and from which they receive pay which doesn't provide for much and which is unlikely to improve. Or, for a few, the city provides an excellent income, which can buy all the nice things. But, this comes at some personal expense - like a willingness to work long hours and produce an expected result (that you have no say in). If either fall off then the compensation falls off as well – so there is a constant stress to maintain the pace!

Urban living also has a vast array of entertainment choices, usually at hefty prices but deemed worth the discomfort of living in a crowded congested environment!

For those who value wide open spaces), the urban setting doesn't work, yet most who feel this way are trapped because it is the only place they can find a job, and without a job, nothing is possible.

There was a time when this was different. People lived in small communities that dotted the country. Many lived in one community for a lifetime. There were likely other family members who lived there as well, and over time many friends were made. There were small businesses that employed people and perhaps, more importantly, if you learned a craft or a trade you could start your own business. Depending on how hard you worked and how clever you were these small business could be quite successful – not so much in terms of becoming a large company (although some did) but certainly in terms of providing well for the family and possibly a few more.

We can talk about earlier times when things were different but there was never a developed plan for America – no blue print no road map. Individuals determined what America would become by making personal decisions as to a course of action for themselves – decisions to move or not move, decisions to build or not build, decisions on what to build, decisions regarding starting a family, decisions on how to best raise that family, how to educate their children, decisions on where to live – in a rural setting or in a community, what kind of community.

These individual decisions led to a culture, which grew into something bigger than the individual families and formed into something workable – communities were formed and began to dot the land and these needed systems and organized approaches to do the things needed to guide and regulate these new communities. Governments appeared to guide these communities – at the community level and then at the progressively larger levels – counties/districts, states, total country.

The question today is, do we need to completely redo everything, or, is there enough to work with given some rededication and course corrections.

Clearly, we have come too far to just wipe the slate clean and start over, and I personally believe there is much to work with; but, like a farmer with a farm that is not productive, we will need to clear what is not useful, re work the land so it can be productive again, add a little fertilizer and plant again, maybe some of the same plants, probably some newer versions. Then we must nurture it, keep the weeds from growing, make sure there is enough water, and at the appropriate time begin to harvest what is growing – in a way that allows for the growth to continue as we harvest.

None of us can figure out how to do this for the total country but we might be able to for our family (like the original people that came to this county) and then we can gather together with some others and rethink/redo our communities. We will need leaders at this point so we will need to take care in determining who should represent us, or even if we ourselves should step out and lead.

It all sounds overwhelming but it didn't stop the original folks who settled this land. They proceeded and by the early part of the 20th century it was clear that they had been successful. Oh, there were aspects not so successful, but for the most part America was clearly the "go to" country in the world and people from all around the world wanted to "come to America".

By ourselves we cannot determine all that is needed to course correct but each of us can think about our own lives and what may need some course correction in order to arrive at our desired destination. This is not greatly different than the challenge the first people coming to America faced. They had some notion of a better life if they came to America so they came and then they had to think about what they had to work with and come up with a plan to survive – which would be a generational plan that their children and grandchildren would either follow or develop their own version of or both. This is how it began, this is how it will continue from here...the question is how to do it in a way that avoids the pitfalls of the past and creates something that is pleasing and that really works!

PART III

WHERE TO FROM HERE?

When a building is cracked and leaning in places, we assume that the foundation is the problem. We have a choice: take down the building and start over; or restore the building. The analogy works for our Nation, it is cracked and leaning in places, but the foundation it was built on is still good, so we must re-imagine a new vision, restore what we can, and build from there!

CHAPTER 9

RE-IMAGINE THE FUTURE – DREAMERS AND VISIONARIES

There was no America before the 1600's except for native Americans – American Indians. Science has pretty well proven that all human life began somewhere in the middle east and that even the so called native people migrated across a land or ice bridge between Russia and Alaska and then to all of North and South America. So, America originally was land - mountains, grasslands, arid land, land with trees, and wild life – animals, birds, fish, etc.

So why did they come? We can only imagine that it had something to do with finding a better life, like food supply, climate, materials to build shelter, etc. Many of the earliest people groups were nomadic, meaning they were always moving, typically following their food supply… animals, fish, plants…it would have taken many, many generations for even a small number of people to come from the Middle East all the way to the western part of Russia, and then on to North and South America. We don't know why they came but we can make a reasonable guess that it was to survive, or find a better way to survive.

So we jump forward to the time when Eurasia was settled and the variety of cultures that encompass that vast area were established. Those cultures are quite different, one from another. Consider just the British Isles: England, Scotland, Wales, and Ireland. Then jump to the mainland of Europe: France, Belgium, Germany, Spain, Italy, Switzerland, etc. It goes on and on. Each is different and each has their own form of government, religious preferences, dress, food, etc. About the only thing that is somewhat the same is football, soccer to us, the international sport, played and enjoyed in virtually all countries.

So why would Europeans want to come to America? My guess is for a reason not a whole lot different from those who migrated much earlier… to find a better life. Or perhaps something in the "old country" didn't appeal to them and was suffocating them, like the religious persecution the Pilgrims experienced; or massive droughts and famines for others, or the class system that existed in that time. Those kinds of things could get someone wondering if there was a better place to live. But where, what would it look like, how would they get there? Apparently, they had some idea about another place, early explorers had been there and brought back information which seemed quite positive and from that a vision was forming; yes, there is a better place, it is called America.

It still amazes me, however, that anyone would risk their life and all that they had to get into a small ship with a few sails and take off for a land they didn't really know anything about. But they did and eventually word got back that It was really a pretty neat place; good land, lots of food, plenty of building materials, precious metals – gold and silver, etc. All of this caused a picture to form in the minds of people about this place called America. It wasn't the same for each person, but yet it kind of was. It was like a vision of something new and appealing. Oh, there were parts not so appealing, like really cold winters, and of course the hard journey to get here during which a few always died; but, in spite of all that, they still came.

And they are still coming! 400 years later America is still the land of promise, the land where you can become whatever you want to become, the land of untold wealth and possibilities, and if only they can get there, they will have it made! Well, we all know that is a stretch but they are still coming. I wonder if the vision of what they are coming for is even remotely the same as it was for those who originally came…probably not. TV and the Internet have changed all that, and the reasons to come probably vary greatly from people group to people group, even from family to family. In effect it is no vision, at least in terms of a national vision.

Vision is something that comes from leadership and the leadership of our nation is not even close to having one, yet it is the first thing a leader should think about. You cannot win if the team is not focused on a common purpose! To put it into biblical terms, *"Where there is no revelation (vision) the people are without restraint"*

So what was the original vision and what should it be today and how should we make it happen? I believe the original vision was a picture of a great land with many wonderful natural assets and opportunities for all and that we will be one big happy family, working together to make our dreams come true! I don't think it was complicated, and it might have been a bit unrealistic. But people came and made the most of it. It was a "melting pot" with each person adding his or her own spice.

A culture emerged that was the key aspect of The United States of America becoming the most powerful Nation on earth. It also was the most generous! Everyone was positive and passionate about America, it was real and it connected everyone. Nothing took away from the traditions that people brought with them from the culture they had left, but it did bring order. The early vision and culture that was emerging guided the development of founding principles from which a National Constitution could be formed:

<u>Popular Sovereignty</u>: The concept that political power rests with the people who can create, alter, and abolish government. People express themselves through voting and free participation in government.

---

* another version says, *the people perish*! Proverbs 29:18

Federalism: A system of government in which a written constitution divides power between a central, or national government and several regional governments.

Limited Government: Everyone, including all authority figures, must obey laws. Constitutions, statements of rights, or other laws define the limits of those in power so they cannot take advantage of the elected, appointed, or inherited positions.

Judicial Review: The power of the Supreme Court to evaluate and declare laws and actions - of local, state, or national government -unconstitutional if necessary. *(Note, it was never intended that they were to make laws – that is the responsibility of congress)*

Separation of Powers: Constitutional division of powers among the legislative, executive, and judicial branches, with the legislative branch making law, the executive applying and enforcing the law, and the judiciary interpreting the law.

Checks and Balances: A system that allows each branch of government to limit the powers of the other branches in order to prevent abuse of power.

These principles are really quite good but it is clear that they aren't exactly being followed – this is where some cracks have appeared. For example; "we, the people", really doesn't have much political power with the emergence of "professional politicians". That may be one of the biggest cracks to develop in the country's foundation over the years. The professional politicians too often function as spoiled, privileged, royal individuals in positions of little or no value that add little, if anything, to the governing needs of our country.

Separation of powers is often ignored when inconvenient, and the Judicial branch sometimes goes beyond their role of just evaluating the constitutionality of laws and actions.

It all seems too complicated to correct! But that is not how one historical leader thought:

Nehemiah, the governor of Jerusalem in 432 B.C. came up with a simple but brilliant solution to rebuild the ruined city after the Persian occupation.

The walls of the city had been knocked down and the massive gates reduced to ashes. This allowed their enemies to ransack the city at will. Nehemiah gave the residents of Jerusalem a mission: "Come, let us rebuild the walls and we will no longer be in disgrace!"

Certainly this wasn't the first time anyone considered this. What they lacked was an effective plan. Nehemiah had one. His plan was for each family to rebuild the portion of the wall next to their house and for shopkeepers to do the same. He had the priests rebuild the sheep gate—special because that was the gate they primarily used. In other words, he asked people to concentrate on rebuilding where they had a personal stake.

So, a leader shows up, captures the attention of the people and gives them a vision, a mission, and a purpose…in one simple statement, "Come, let us rebuild…and we will no longer be in disgrace". He followed that up with such a brilliant plan that it is often missed…it was brilliant in its simplicity and brilliant in its capability to immediately enroll all of the people. Why? Because he asked them to handle the repair of the cracked and fallen wall by repairing the portion next to their house! Who would know that portion of the wall and how to do it right better than the people who lived next to it?

The ownership on the part of everyone was 'over the top', it's clear from the rest of the story: the wall and gates of Jerusalem were totally rebuilt or repaired in fifty-two days. You may have seen that wall, I have and it's not small, it's huge, and in a time where there was no power equipment, fifty two days is unimaginable – but it's true. It was a result of brilliant leadership willing to engage the people in a meaningful way – that rarely happens in our world today but when it does, look out!

A modern Exodus

In 1972 my family and I moved to the State of Georgia – facilitated by The Procter and Gamble Company, my employer. I was in the early years of my career as a manufacturing manager and we were building a new facility in the southern part of the state to make Pampers disposable diapers, Charmin bathroom tissue and Bounty paper towels, all a part of the expansion of their paper products business. I didn't realize it at the time but our move coincided with the exodus of the US population from rural settings to urban settings. The hub city for Georgia is, of course, Atlanta, 200 miles to the north. At the time of our move the population of the metro area was about a million people. As I write this book, 45 years later, the population is about six million and growing. There are pluses and minuses to the transformation this has caused but all in all, it's an exciting place to live.

There are several drivers of this growth! First, Atlanta is the hub of the southeast and to some extent an intercontinental hub given that the busiest airport in the world is located there along with 3 major interstate highways; I 20, I 75 and I 85. It is a city of "headquarter companies", 26 at last count, 16 of them fortune 500 companies: Delta Airlines, Home Depot, UPS, Coke, Aflac, Southern Company, Suntrust, Mohawk, NCR, Chick fil-A to name some. Additionally Atlanta is the largest film/movie production city in the world; at last count there were 100 studios in the state, mostly the Atlanta region.

This became a possibility when Ted Turner began CNN and his string of media companies. That introduced the skill of filmmaking which many craft oriented people have taken advantage of – to learn and become film technicians of various forms. As this was taking place Hollywood producers began to take advantage of the lower cost opportunity to make portions of their films and that has grown to the point of several film companies establishing studios, resulting in several thousand jobs becoming available – from producers to actors to technicians of all types.

Another growth factor is the climate and the fact that many varieties of trees and shrubbery grow well in the region making Atlanta a "city in the forest". Over the years care has been taken to preserve trees as much as possible, even at the expense of sub optimizing highway development which has led to another issue (to be discussed further on); but the location, the trees and a climate that allows 300 days of golf a year are certainly an attraction. The following article by Jeanne Bonner appeared in the November 2017 issue of Delta airlines monthly magazine SKY:

> *A "City in the Forest", a southern city with a climate that allows for 300 days of golf each year. Its topography varies widely: multiple business districts dotted with high rise buildings right next to residential neighborhoods full of postcard-ready Victorian cottages, plus wooded areas with creeks and suburban shopping plazas, often with under-the –radar eateries.*
>
> *It's no surprise that the city is home to one of America's most ambitious urban redevelopment projects; the "Atlanta Beltline", when completed, this 33-mile walking and biking loop will link 15 of Atlanta's parks and 45 of its neighborhoods. But it's more than a path; the project has added new green space to the city and spurred massive retail and residential development.*

Atlanta has progressed from being nearly destroyed in the civil war a hundred and fifty years earlier to a vibrant and attractive place to live. Many, like us, have moved to the region for the reasons described.

Other cities in the region such as Savannah and Brunswick have benefited from this growth as well, stimulated by the fact that both cities have become important "port cities" with a steady build up of capacity for "container ships" and the need for more roads and trucks to carry the incoming and outgoing cargos to and from locations all across the eastern states and beyond.

Other cities in the region have benefited from automobile assembly plants and the supporting businesses making parts. The landscape from Greenville, South Carolina to Montgomery, Alabama reveals a major shift from the "rust belt" to the "sun belt" for heavy manufacturing. The 350-mile radius around Atlanta contains several other medium size – and growing cities including Birmingham, Alabama; Charlotte, North Carolina; Charleston, South Carolina; and Jacksonville Florida. We have mentioned Savannah and Brunswick but also the cities close to Atlanta – Columbus and Macon – are important to the growth of the region as well.

But as this exodus has continued it could be argued that the growth is more of a detriment than an asset. There are issues needing attention with the most prominent being: congested highways, a school system that doesn't provide a quality education for the development of young people in this new landscape, and several "out of sight" neighborhoods where poverty, poor health and crime continue.

This growth, and the fact that 80% of the population are now living in cities have given a new face to America generally and Atlanta specifically. But part of the new face does not contain the work force of earlier years – The rugged, can do, entrepreneur/leaders and craft oriented workers that can make things happen.

Oh, buildings are being built, new roads squeezed in, entertainment venues added, but the result is not complete in terms of things like pleasant communities and schools, and green space to grow up, live, and feel safe in, and transportation capability to get to wherever we need or want to go.

People in general, from elected officials, business leaders and local community leaders are confused about many things. It seems like new rules and norms about what can be said or done is changing from the principles and values that have been the stabilizer right from the beginning of the country's formation. The result is a growing level of dissention that causes an inability to move forward on many things.

It has become clearer and clearer that America is less than perfect, and more and more obvious that significant changes are needed. The primary problem seems to be a breakdown of leadership at the top, which has led to a host of problems economically, culturally and spiritually. As grandparents Kathie and I have become more and more concerned about what our children will be left with – just what kind of mess will it be?

As I write this in 2018 there are some hopeful things happening even though the country's leaders are embroiled in disagreement for almost everything. This is a series of disagreements that basically started at the beginning of the new presidential term that began in January of 2018. My intent is to neither evaluate what is happening nor predict its outcome. Surely no one wants to stay in this current reality, all of us want to move on to a future state that continues to follow the principles and practices that truly has made America great, and to do that there does need to be some course corrections to arrive at the future state we all desire to have. What could that look like?

Desired Future State 2030 – A Vision

The ten-year period starting in 2020 has turned out to be almost magical in the development of several things ranging from an overhaul of our education approach to transportation advances never dreamed possible to advances economically that have provided the funds to totally rework total low income communities to no longer be "low income!" Of course this hasn't happened overnight and it is still a "work in progress" but it is working so well and is so encouraging that the "No Sayers" and critics have turned into advocates to help lead the rest of the population. To say there are no remaining problems would be an overstatement but, clearly, a way forward has been found and there is likely no one who is not encouraged.

How has this happened? Well, it started when we became more of one mind politically. No, not one party, we still have more than one, in fact we have several, but in order for any one to have a say there has to be some connecting done to increase the vote size. As this became obvious a very interesting thing happened. Our population in general began to see value in "working to agree", in other words, to "find consensus". Oh, it's not to the point of everyone agreeing; but it has developed enough agreement to create a block of votes that allow action! This action has provided the impetus to move forward on several things that had been just points of discussion in prior years – there was never enough support, and frankly just too much useless argument that led to nothing! So it's like a new light got turned on for our general population and it has been enough to get the support needed to move forward.

There were two areas in the beginning that received the needed attention and funding support. One was **transportation** and the other **education**. Here is what happened:

First, attention was given to the development of "high speed' rail to connect the population centers of the south with Atlanta, the hu. Right along with that the road system was changed to separate cars and trucks, which allowed bigger trucks (lower costs) and smoother commutes for people. This included the addition of more elevated roads as well as underground roads plus a greatly expanded "city train system" that connected all the other systems.

The result was clear in terms of an easier commute for working people as well as all others who before would rarely venture past their home turf. Driverless car technology has flourished, and the truck roads have supported a whole new way of thinking about distribution of products at much lower cost and that has spurred economic growth – adding to the economic well being of the region in general and each family in particular.

Before this, Atlanta had been a city in which several companies established their headquarters, due largely to the position of the city as a hub; however, a negative that caused some to go elsewhere had been the congestion of the road system. Once this system was working, it became a very positive factor in the establishment of several more "head quarters" and adding to the economic and lifestyle vitality of the area overall!

This has also spurred the reimagining and rebuilding of whole neighborhoods, which in turn provides jobs and income to the families of these neighborhoods. Along with this, positive changes and additions to the health care system as well as care of the poor and disabled have occurred and are finally providing what is needed. While difficult to achieve perfection recent surveys indicate an approval rating of 90%

As all of this has taken place another very key area of need is being addressed: Education. It was realized that this couldn't be thought of as just the "school system". The education of our youth had to be considered in light of what the future is likely to look like and in 2020 that was fuzzy at best, plus it was just hard to see past the problems and issues of the current reality. Slowly, the same "aha's" mentioned earlier occurred: that we needed to find others of like mind (perhaps similar mind), and figure out how to move forward.

But to move forward we had to understand where we were currently. After some argument it was decided to examine the "current reality" in a way that was not biased and could provide a good starting place.

It took some time but eventually a reasonably good picture of where we are today emerged and, although not perfect, it was embraced to be good enough to proceed. After all this was not the vision for the future but rather a picture of what we wanted to leave. Here is a composite of the "current reality" of education in America" in the year 2020:

- There is no concise picture – rather widely different approaches from home schools to private schools to public schools

- It doesn't address what people will do after their school years for the most part; therefore it doesn't prepare them

- Too much of a "one size fits all" when the reality is that each student is unique and needs to have the opportunity to develop uniquely.

- It varies from teacher to teacher and school to school, etc. It is widely variable, no consistency

- It is often flavored by the one doing the teaching – and widely inconsistent from very good to very bad, and typically, little to no understanding of these differences by the administrative leadership, or worse, influenced by them to be variable

- We have lost the rigor and discipline needed to learn the basics, the three R'S: Reading, Riting (Writing) and Rithmetic (Arithmetic/Math).

- We underutilize the one to one relationship aspect of learning: parenting, apprenticeship, coaching, mentoring

- We underappreciate (therefore underutilize) the aspect of summer/part time jobs or other ways to do work/learning internships

- School programs tend to be time consuming and inefficient

- Home schooling can be efficient but it tends to lack the resources needed

- We tend to value getting a young person through secondary school and college so they can move on instead of factoring in initial jobs as part of the education

- Our progress measurement approaches are typically inefficient and in effective

From this a sweeping vision/purpose statement was created that would give the general direction of where we would try to go with our thinking to reset this very important bar:

A cradle to grave approach for learning and development that is easily accessible and available for all people of all ages and interests and financial capability – monitored and facilitated by trained professionals along with a cadre of volunteers who can easily and effectively participate via a smooth and understandable system

Of course that statement is too general to be useful in creating a way forward so we added some strategic statements that suggest how to get there:

1. *Learning the basics: 3 R's etc. in the elementary/middle school years*
2. *Going deeper in more advanced course work: secondary schools, colleges, training institutions of all kinds*
3. *Apprenticeship/internships for a wide variety of things, especially craft and hand skills*
4. *raining/learning venues for job/career changes*
5. *Career development/change approaches*
6. *Understanding seasons of life (family, jobs, locations, age, etc) and how to prepare for them*

With this serving as a direction we created several situations to test in the Atlanta region, which included all of north Georgia. We involved a wide range of people to help run and evaluate the tests: parents, educators, students, business people, essentially a good representation of individuals involved in youth development in general. The results of these tests were used to begin organizing an initial approach that was tested in various locations throughout the Atlanta region.

Those tests were then used to refine and further develop the approach that has been identified. There were several iterations of this before we were comfortable with moving to the next phase, which was to start up 6 test sites with the identified approach. The plan for this was to run the test sites for a year and measure results. Another iteration of the approach was completed and we equipped the test sites with this revision. At this point we were 4 years into the effort and planned to move forward in all communities of the region. Our expectation was to run with our resulting approach for 2 years before making any more revisions.

At that point we made one more set of revisions based on the results thus far and continued. That was 4 years ago and now ten years after we started we are very pleased with the results:

- Participation levels (no child left behind): 90%
- High approval ratings from parents (90%) for education in general on recent surveys
- Huge improvement (20-30%) on college entrance testing
- Over 90% enrolled in college, joined the military, or found a job by age 20

Vision summary:

So what is the point? The point is that America has been the nation of dreamers and visionary thinking and it still is – it is alive and well and can be seen in many places just as we are seeing it in Atlanta. I believe the above vision will happen, it is already underway in cities and metropolitan areas all across the country. Over the course of the next 10 years much will change in this country, most for the good, some perhaps not so good…but 2030 will look different than 2018 in many ways! The question for each of us is what is our role in it all, can we help focus it, and can we have a piece of the action in some way?? Much of what does occur in our country occurs through the political and business processes and that needs some adjustments to be really successful in my mind. That is the topic of the next chapters.

CHAPTER 10

RESTORE WHAT CAN BE RESTORED GOVERNMENT

Government

On April 9,1865, Robert E Lee surrendered at Appomattox Courthouse ending the Civil War and the most divisive and destructive time our Nation has ever experienced. If left to continue there would be no *America* as we know it today. Abraham Lincoln was our president and he led the country out of that debacle and then died from an assassin's bullet 6 days later on April 15th. His leadership during this most difficult time produced a path for reconciliation and ultimately the opportunity to become the World Power that it became by the end of World War II, in 1945 – 80 years later!

On November 19, 1863, following the battle of Gettysburg, Lincoln addressed a crowd of some 15,000 people. He spoke for less than two minutes, and the entire speech was only 272 words long. Beginning by invoking the image of the founding fathers and the new nation, Lincoln eloquently expressed his conviction that the Civil War was the ultimate test of whether the Union created in 1776 would survive, or "perish from the earth." The dead at Gettysburg had laid down their lives for this noble cause, he said, and it was up to the living to confront the "great task" before them: ensuring that *"government of the people, by the people, for the people, shall not perish from the earth."*

The Gettysburg Address

Four score and seven years ago our fathers brought forth on this continent, a new nation, conceived in Liberty, and dedicated to the proposition that all men are created equal.

Now we are engaged in a great civil war, testing whether that nation, or any nation so conceived and so dedicated, can long endure. We are met on a great battlefield of that war. We have come to dedicate a portion of that field, as a final resting place for those who here gave their lives that that nation might live. It is altogether fitting and proper that we should do this.

*But, in a larger sense, we cannot dedicate—we cannot consecrate—we cannot hallow—this ground. The brave men, living and dead, who struggled here, have consecrated it, far above our poor power to add or detract. The world will little note, nor long remember what we say here, but it can never forget what they did here. It is for us the living, rather, to be dedicated here to the unfinished work, which they who fought here have thus far so nobly advanced. It is rather for us to be here dedicated to the great task remaining before us—that from these honored dead we take increased devotion to that cause for which they gave the last full measure of devotion—that we here highly resolve that these dead shall not have died in vain—**that this nation, under God, shall have a new birth of freedom—and that government of the people, by the people, for the people, shall not perish from the earth.***

Abraham Lincoln November 19, 1863

Of the principles stated in Chapter 9 there are two that I believe Lincoln was referring to with his phrase *government of the people, by the people, for the people…*

The Principle above called <u>Federalism:</u> a system of government in which power is distributed between a central or national government and several regional governments

The principle called <u>Popular Sovereignty</u>: that political power rests with the people who can create, alter, and abolish government. People express themselves in voting and free participation in government.

Taken together these express what I believe could be a major solution for many of the difficulties we experience in our government today. The exact opposite is happening as power is now concentrated, more than ever, at the National level; and to take it further, it is concentrated specifically at the Executive branch of that level. States have been overridden on several counts in recent times and communities, families and individuals are left to pick up the pieces, which typically amounts to, "just suck it up!"

To correct this we ***must continue to*** <u>elect</u> new leadership who will return us to the excellence we are capable of …this must be priority one! It isn't a structural issue in my mind, it is a distribution of power issue, which can be rectified by a national government leadership that has the right people in the right place to vote effectively for measures to reallocate this power.

As we do this we must take care to learn all we can about the candidates that are running for office and pick those who truly represent us, that walk the talk everyday just as we do…and to ignore those that get to where they are by "Knowing the right people" and buying their way in. We also need to enact legislation that limits the length of terms for all elected officials to force fresh learning as new individuals are elected particularly to the Senate and House of Representatives. Those seem to be the governmental bodies that house the professional politicians.

Along with this the rules regarding Lobbyists and influence tactics used need to be carefully reviewed and reformed to reduce and level these aspects of political life that seem to be the primary tools of the professional politicians, especially practices regarding funding and the granting of special roles.

The question, once the right people are in office, is what should be worked on and to what end? I have many thoughts and ideas but so does everyone else. The reason to elect those who truly represent us is that is the best possibility to have what we want and need for our lives in terms of the way of our government functions to make it happen. By and large, I think that once we have leaders we trust and honest effort to accomplish any variety of things, most of us can leave it to these elected people to take care of it. That leaves us to take care of business or life in general in our own neck of the woods in the best way we deem necessary, a much more efficient use of everyone's time when you think about it.

I suspect there will always be those in our population that will not be ok with this approach and they will want to voice their own ideas in some way – certainly that should be allowed as long as its within the law and to some extent our cultural norms (even that can be questioned if done lawfully and perhaps even tastefully)

Business

I believe business has generally missed on an important aspect of their process – the people aspect. I remember that about 20-25 years ago, as the industrial age was diminishing and the information age was taking off, there seemed to be a conscious effort to not repeat the lessons of 'smokestack industry' as it was sometimes referred to. The belief of those information age pioneers, who did some truly remarkable things, was that to move forward they must not pay too much attention to the way those earlier monster organizations functioned. While there was some truth to what they thought – there were certainly things not to repeat – I do believe there was the beginning of a movement in several of the mega companies regarding people and how best to lead them that was essentially ignored.

I'm talking about the movement that began in the 1970's and 80's to develop team approaches in the organization and coaching techniques in the leadership. I'm aware that those terms are commonly used today, but that is where it stops typically, I see very little application occurring. What I do see is leaders who are there only because they started the company, or leaders who are the brainiest technician or architect, and of course leaders who are focused on their own deal and how much they will personally benefit. I don't see very many leaders who really know how to tap the vast resource that exists in their workers. Certainly there are some but I don't see many who can encourage and motivate their people, and I don't see leaders who understand organizational culture and what makes it powerful and what destroys it.

It follows then that organizations are not much different than the Frederick Taylor influenced organizations of the early 20th century. Many are essentially "box like" jobs; the work is an advanced level of technical work from that earlier time, to be sure, but still by an individual in a box. They were called hourly workers or operators or mechanics/ electricians; now, increasingly, they are called "contractors" or perhaps "consultants". Yes there are other terms used; software developers, software architects, etc. and there are still marketing and sales people, research and development people, and other special function people who are called in accordance with the name of the function.

There were many places in industry where progress was being made on this subject – I was with one of them, Procter and Gamble, and during my more recent consulting years I have learned of more. I wrote a chapter in my book "Back to the Cottage" called *The Design*. That chapter is reprinted here in the addendum and provides a way of thinking regarding large organizations (or smaller ones for that matter).

What follows is another illustration of a way of thinking regarding organizational design in the information age. This is a company that has started and progressed to a global entity in the past 20 years. I will not identify them nor will I describe their business, but I will describe some of the aspects and principles being used for their organizational design. None of this is "made up", it is real and it works

> Integrated product offerings: The company has determined that the software development and accounting components of the business plan could be integrated with the primary product offerings to create a more full offering to customers. With this in mind the design of the organization has taken on a multi faceted team structure with all components represented. This requires cross-functional understanding on the part of all members of the organization to make the teams most effective. This is not knew but important to understand the rest.

> Multifunctional teams with multifunctional individuals: Each person is trained and developed not only in the specific expertise they bring (software development, accounting expertise, client interaction, project management, etc) but also skills that relate to a variety of relationships needed for the business team to be successful, such as customer and supplier interaction, and cross functional interaction across the company. Specially skilled individuals (who normally would not be called on to interact with a client/customer) interact regularly with customers in terms of their expertise, which increases the value of what the company offers. This is recognized and valued by the customers, and it is especially recognized and valued by the employees of the company. The company does contract some work but minimally and typically in the region of their growing global reach.

> Flat organizational structure: Very few levels with much of the leadership within the teams handled by individuals who have shown leadership capability along with their base expertise; ie, Journeymen and Journeywomen. This occurs on an as needed basis; ie, a new project, a special task team, training a new person(s), a company committee representative, etc.

➢ Team leaders for those teams that are primary to the core process of the company are selected from the journeymen and journeywomen and given further development opportunities (training, special assignments, etc) to add to their already demonstrated capabilities. One of the key approaches are workshops which engage several leaders (six to ten) to interact around a variety of case study type situations and, in effect, learn from each other. Another approach is the use of coaches and mentor. These are not assigned, but they are encouraged and each individual has freedom to pick who they would like from the coaches and mentors who are more experienced.

➢ Rewards across the company are based on the contribution each person makes each year as evaluated by some basic metrics (targets set at the beginning of the year) along with the results of each person's efforts to develop other individuals and teams. It is not a system that necessarily provides the greatest reward to the person with the most people reporting to them or the largest number of whatever is measured…unless that is perceived to be the largest contribution overall, all things considered!

➢ Careful attention is paid to both the lack of hierarchy and the contribution based reward system. The company feels that the lack of "position and hierarchy" keeps the "vying for position" issue – that can so often plague an organization - under control.

➢ When someone visits this business one of their takeaways is their observation of the culture and how positive it is. Likewise, whenever I talk with a new person, recently recruited – the primary reason for their decision to join was their observation of the positive nature of the culture along with the intelligence of the people. It is a hard thing to measure but how important would it be for any company to have an organizational culture that attracts the best of the best and at the same time can interact with a customer or a supplier in a way that says "we are the best" even without saying it!

To summarize, If we can get back to the original principles from which our Nation was founded, especially the part about the involvement of the people and if we can begin to evolve the organizations in the Market place to be more about the development and involvement of their internal people, we would, at a minimum be tapping a whole lot more God created brainpower that we are today. It would be like it originally was in America, when you think about it – on a much larger scale to be sure, but when you break it down to workable units – it is indeed possible!

Community

There is a pretty amazing truth that exists in America; *communities come together to help each other in a time of difficulty, tragedy, or loss.* This is a characteristic that is special to our culture and not as true in most of the rest of the world. What makes this so? I believe it has to do with how our culture came to be in the first place.

American culture has always been a result of the people working together to forge a place to live – From the very beginning! Starting with the first settlements and continuing through the westward migration, a civil war, two world wars, and the immigration of millions from other countries and nationalities. It was called a "melting pot" as different people groups came together to build communities.

Imagine the characteristics that were forged as this took place! A *willingness to work together* because "Two are better than one, and a cord of three strands is not easily broken"! It is like the Nehemiah story where each family worked on the wall next to their house and when it came to protecting what they were building they banned together to protect the city (Nehemiah chapters 2 – 6); In the same way the *need for protection and security* also factored into those early characteristics of communities in our new country. To this day they can be seen any time a tornado, flood or fire hits!

This is true in most communities but not all. There are communities that have been hit by another storm – an economic one that develops quietly but surely. It happens in a variety of ways – companies moving - or failing - causing jobs to disappear and forcing people to move to other communities to find work.

Ethnic polarization can also influence people to ignore one another at the expense of not solving problems that are of concern to each. These are opportunities that require the talents of the potential journeymen and women amongst them to take the first steps of connecting and finding the common ground to build on, like working together to recruit new businesses with the promise of an excellent work force that will do excellent work! This is likely no different than what had to happen in earlier years of our history. It wasn't a politician nor was it a successful investor/entrepreneur that pulled the people of a community together. It was the average citizen with a journey man/woman mentality; and not just one, but several who collectively said, we need to fix this, and we need to rally the citizenry of our community to help us do what needs to be done.

To conclude, chapter 9 is about Dreamers and Visionaries *Reimagining* the future, how it would look, and how to accomplish it. Chapter 10 is about restoring what I'm referring to as Journeymen and women to the place of *leading by doing* – doing the work needed to govern or to restore and rebuild communities, businesses, roads and bridges, etc. There is no huge cache of gold and silver nor is there a magic potion, but we don't need any of that. We have a far greater resource, our citizens. Within those ranks is everything we need, every idea, every skill, and every solution.

Our communities and the talent that resides within, from dreamers and visionaries to Journey-men and women are the reason for our national success, and it is also the target of enemies we can't always see, from corrupt ideologies to our own unwillingness to connect and find the common ground on which to build!

CHAPTER 11

BUILD WHAT IS
NOT YET THERE

My original thought re Journeymen was to capture in words what my experience has been regarding the journeymen I've known, starting with my own father and then those I have met along the way.

The concept started with men I saw in the work place that were "difference makers"; that is they, as one person, made the difference on a team to be great as opposed to average. I would say to Jim Collins ...the author of "Good to Great" that perhaps the most important factor in addition to what he describes (and I take no issue with any of that) would be journeymen. Throughout American history they have been the difference I believe, not for the vision typically, but for the execution of the strategies needed to reach that vision; and, it is usually not just one person, but several who collaborate and encourage all the others to join in that makes anything really go forward!

Work the following to fit – as if this is a missing element that need to take care to "build into our private lives – it's not a gov't program or a business or any thing _ the question is where are we on the two things God had against the Israelites – if we are guilty of drinking our of our own cistern then perhaps it would be wise to correct that!!!???

As I've studied the subject and considered what is really true about a journeyman is that although the word originally meant a person who had made the journey to achieve a level of excellence in a particular craft, the reality is that a true journeyman would be one who has made the life journey in such a way for us to say, "that man has finished the journey and is worthy of the statement, 'well done, thy good and faithful servant'" (Jesus words in the Parable of the Talents - Matthew 25:21… He goes on to say "you have been faithful with a few things, I will put you in charge of many things"). This verse describes the Journeyman well I believe: They start out in a learning mode and probably make plenty of mistakes in the beginning – both in terms of learning a skill but also in terms of life issues in general, raising a family, becoming involved in their community, etc. In fact, that is the journey. Along the way he begins to think about life in broader terms perhaps in a spiritual way and the way the Bible refers to us as being sons and daughters of God, and the verse, "Whoever hears my words and believes Him who sent me, has eternal life" John 5:24. I coach a lot of men professionally and its not unusual for them to describe to me a pattern of realizing these things, pondering them for a time and then beginning to make life decisions with them in mind as they progress through the years.

It was this way for me, I was 30 years old when I started thinking about verses in the Bible like these, and wondering what they meant for me, were they for real? I'll jump ahead and tell you that I determined they were and, though it didn't change the direction I was going, it sure added an element that I have found to be encouraging and pleasing. There is another verse that I find helpful "be anxious for nothing, but in everything, with gratefulness, make you requests known to God and the peace that passes all understanding will guard your heart and your mind in Christ Jesus". As these and other thoughts have penetrated my life I have become more award of His presence in my life and am eternally grateful for His leading. The next piece is a powerful expression of who He is and what He wishes for all of us.

Buy a Field

The Book of Jeremiah in the Old Testament Bible records a series of prophesies by a man named Jeremiah regarding the destruction of Jerusalem by the Babylonians, and the exile of those living there to Babylonia for a period of 70 years. The reason for this was the continued failure on the part of the Jews to follow God, even though, in an earlier time, He had brought them out of Egypt to this "Promised Land"(Israel).

This is what the Lord says: "What fault did your fathers find in me, that they strayed so far from me? They followed worthless idols and became worthless themselves. They did not ask, 'Where is the Lord who brought us up out of Egypt and led us through the barren wilderness, a land of deserts and rifts, a land of drought and darkness, a land where no one travels and no one lives?'" Jeremiah 2: 5-6

"I brought you into a fertile land to eat its fruit and rich produce. But you came and defiled my land and made my inheritance detestable. The priests did not ask, 'Where is the Lord?' Those who deal with the law did not know me. The prophets prophesied by Baal, following worthless idols." Jeremiah: 2: 7-8

"Therefore, I bring charges against you again," declares the Lord, "and I will bring charges against your children's children." Jeremiah 2:5-9

"My people have committed two sins: They have forsaken me, the spring of living water, and have dug their own cisterns (gone their own way)." Jeremiah 2:13

"To all the people of Judah and Jerusalem…I have spoken to you again and again but you have not listened." Jeremiah 25: 2-3

"Therefore…because you have not listened…I will summon the people of the North and Nebuchadnezzar, King of Babylon…to completely destroy them (Jerusalem and Judah)…this country will become a desolate wasteland and these people will serve the king of Babylon seventy years." Jeremiah 25 8-11

And then God, again through the prophet Jeremiah, says, *"When seventy years are completed for Babylon, I will come to you and fulfill my promise to bring you back to this place. For I know the plans I have for you...plans to prosper you and not to harm you, plans to give you hope and a future. Then you will call upon me...you will seek me...and I will be found by you...and I will bring you back from captivity." Jeremiah 29: 10-14.*

This is part of the incredible story of God and His "chosen people" the nation of Israel to whom he also said, *"I will give them a heart to know me, that I am the Lord. They will be my people and I will be their God!" Jeremiah 24:7*

In chapter 2 (Journeyman) I mentioned Nehemiah, a man that I think of as a journeyman. He was born as a slave during this period of exile prophesied by Jeremiah. In young adulthood he was specifically the slave who served the King his wine. He was obviously a man who could be trusted and as it turns out, a man of eventual leadership capability. When he hears about his ancestral home, Jerusalem, destroyed 70 years earlier by the Babylonians, he is overcome by emotion and grief.

The king, Ataxerxes, notices and asks what's wrong. Nehemiah answers truthfully about what he is hearing about Jerusalem and his desire to do something to help. The King says ok and not only releases Nehemiah to go to Jerusalem, he sends him as governor with a cadre of others to help along with materials to rebuild when they get there. I mentioned earlier the brilliance he demonstrates once there and the speed of rebuilding that occurs.

Let's stop and consider what is going on here:

God is not pleased with the people of Judah and Jerusalem for two primary reasons: He says; *they have forsaken me - and - they have gone their own way!*

Jeremiah prophesies the destruction of Jerusalem and the exile of the people there to Babylonia for a period of 70 years. He also prophesies God saying ...*When seventy years are completed...I will bring you back!*

Seventy years later Nehemiah emerges to lead the rebuilding of Jerusalem!

In many ways I see America in these verses. First of all, I believe God ordained that we be here. You can see it in our history, and I believe we can, in a way, feel it – we feel a spirit of something that is unlike any other country in the world. And we can see it – in the events that have occurred over the centuries that we have been here, many that can only be explained as God's hand protecting and God's hand blessing.

There have been some up's and down's, but American's have risen to the task and made difficult things into positive outcomes; and, for the most part we have thanked God and looked to Him for the next steps. We as a nation have been humble enough to know that it wasn't us but He who turned the tide, who gave the invention, who paved the way!

In recent years, however, something changed: *As a culture we seem less dedicated to the reality that we need God,* certainly not to the point of the early Americans for over 350 years – up to about 1960! It was then that our collective desire for God's protection and blessing began to wane, for all of the reasons already stated.

Personally, I believe we can course correct, but we need to get started soon. I've listed my own thoughts in the previous chapters but I've saved the most important thing for last.

We can do all of the things above plus many more that others will suggest, and we can do it all with the best of human capability we have as a nation – and that capability is phenomenal; but, if we continue to do it without the leading and the protection of Our Father in Heaven, it will be for naught and we may well find ourselves exiled – maybe for seventy years, like the people of Jerusalem.

But if we… *trust in the Lord with all our hearts, and lean <u>not</u> on our own understanding, and rather, in all our ways, acknowledge Him, <u>then</u> He will make our paths straight (Proverbs 3; 5,6).* That's what he did for Nehemiah and the people of Judah and Jerusalem – I believe He would love to do it for us! To do this we must assure that we are electing governing representatives that will follow God in like manner; at the very least enough of them to become a majority and provide the overall leadership needed for America to become great once again, not great in power only, but great in the power of God.

I continue to think that what I said above may be right, even the Babylonian exile. Some say that America is the modern day version of Babylonia - you can certainly see many similarities. As I've pondered this and thought about the downward slide of America, it seems to have begun in the 50's and 60's but you can find at least one early root in 1935 when Roosevelt's Social Security act was enacted, then again in 1945 when it became clear that America was *The* world power...I wonder if the seed was planted then. God could have stopped the events that began taking place then, the social revolution that included the outlawing of God's word in schools and eventually all public places, along with government approval for murdering innocent children yet in the womb...and on and on to where we are now – some 70 years since we became *The* world power!!

Interesting – perhaps God has already had us serving the king of Babylon for 70 years???

And perhaps He will "Bring us back"?

I find chapter 32 of Jeremiah very interesting. He tells Jeremiah to **buy a field** from his cousin and in verse 15 it says: *For this is what the Lord Almighty, the God of Israel, says: Houses, fields and vineyards **will again be bought in this land.***

He goes on to say in verse 33: *They turned their backs to me and not their faces, though I taught them again and again, they would not listen or respond to discipline...*

And verse 36: *But this is what the Lord says: I will surely gather them from all the lands where I banished them in my furious anger and great wrath; I will bring them back to this place and let them live in safety. They will be my people and I will be their God.*

Verse 43: *Once more fields will be bought in this land…*

And to repeat Jeremiah 29:10–14, *This is what the Lord says: When seventy years are completed for Babylon, I will come to you and fulfill my promise…For I know the plans I have for you, declares the Lord, plans to prosper you and not to harm you, plans to give you hope and a future. Then you will call on me and come and pray to me and I will listen to you. You will seek me and find me when you seek me with all your heart. I will be found by you, declares the Lord, and will bring you back from captivity.*

Certainly, this was a word from the Lord to the Israelites of a different time, but like many things in the Word of God, it expresses God's heart toward His people. He does discipline but He also loves us and restores us!

With this in mind allow me to share the following:

A. In my youth – 1945 – 1965 – I experienced a way of life that earlier was labeled, *The Cottage Age*! I grew up in a remnant of that age and I experienced:

- Small businesses that can evolve and be successful enough to support a couple of families and provide jobs (full and part time) for several more people and their families
- Small businesses that are based around a home and interconnected with other home based businesses.
- Small farms that provide food for the family that owns it plus more from the overflow that can be produced.
- Local trade of a variety of goods and services via barter (trade without the use of money)
- Families with members (Mom and Dad mostly) that possessed a skill (s) passed down generationally.
- An almost perfect environment to start (teach and develop) the next generation

B. A few years ago my wife and I vacationed in Vermont. While there we visited the small town of Cabot. Several years prior to our visit the local Creamery where the famers brought their milk was about to shut down – it was losing money. The area farmers pooled their money and bought the creamery – which saved it but did not make it profitable. To make it profitable they had to find a way to get more money for their milk. The solution was to turn the milk into cheese – not just any cheese, a really good cheese - and they appropriately name the cheese after the town…Cabot Cheese is now famous as one of the best cheddar cheeses on the market, earning it the right to be priced very competitively – not enough to make everyone that participated in the coop wealthy, but enough to preserve the small farm culture they had enjoyed for generations.

In an adjacent town another effort was taking place to create a similar coop approach for maple syrup – a natural product that goes back to the beginning of our Nation. Maple Syrup, like corn, was passed along to the early Americans by the native Indians and became a secondary source of income as well as sugar supply to those northeastern farmers down through the years. Not to be outdone by the creativity to increase the value of milk they found ways to create a variety of offshoot products from the syrup – one of the primary ones is a line of salad dressings supplied nationally to a variety of stores – both regular food stores and specialty shops.

When I saw all of this I was both excited and sad – excited at the prospect of this kind of thinking and the American life style it preserved, but sad that we didn't think of this in my home community – It was similar in terms of small farms - milk and maple syrup. Unfortunately this kind of thinking did not occur and the area today is pretty desolate with unfarmed farms, and young people have left for a lack of work opportunities (The big box stores never came other than an occasional Kmart or Wal-Mart – but that was enough to close down most of the other small stores, leaving not much of anything really).

C. There seems to be the beginning of a movement in many parts of our country in the direction of more wholesome foods that will forge healthier lifestyles, reduce the over weight reality of a large percentage of our population, and at the same time create a new economic engine, albeit small. This is occurring in the form of a variety of self-help programs as well as organically grown foods of all kinds. For the most part it's an expensive way to go but the trend surely seems to be upward; and, as demand grows either the price will goes up or the supply increase - or both.

The point is this is a growing market opportunity, small for now – maybe quite large eventually – This, coupled with the lack of appreciation for foreign grown and foreign made goods, may provide the impetus for new investment thinking and strategy.

It won't happen overnight – there will need to be experiments and tests to determine the viability of such endeavors and it certainly won't turn our nation around overnight. But it is inevitable that these experiments and tests will be made (just like the dairy farms in Vermont). Some will prove doable and profitable and they will grow, others will fall by the roadside to make room for the next effort.

America is an entrepreneurial country; there is no doubt that this will be a future reality until the Lord returns. Until that occurs He who created us in his image – creative as He is creative, will always be trying to find a better way!

So here is my question – what will it take to get moving? One direction may be the direction of the Vermont example. Certainly that could be done in other communities. But there are no remnants left to start from - no small farms or small creameries from which to begin.

Several years ago there was a Procter and Gamble Chairman of the Board who was fond of saying, "you can take all of our product formulas, all of our manufacturing capacity, all of our buildings, even all of our money…but leave us our people and we will rebuild this company in 3 years".

My wife and I are moving to a small community south of Atlanta this summer. I've noticed that they have already formed a community watch organized approach and they regularly check with each other about all kinds of things; what brand of food to buy, how to treat a bee sting, what to do about the tracks in someone's yard where a careless teenager ran across a corner of the yard. I'm sure there are many more things like this – the point is they are beginning to co-op their understanding about things important to them. I can imagine this turning into all kinds of things particularly regarding food supply and security in particular.

What if this community was "to buy a field", say a hundred acres or more and then recruit a farm family to come and run the farm – perhaps it would be a dairy, perhaps vegetables, perhaps goats and chickens? An all purpose building could be located on the property (or two or three) to house the farm operations including some value added products like cheese, etc …and maybe a store where additional local made products (furniture, etc) could be sold. More people would be needed – some from the community, others recruited to get the special skills needed to start more things. More land and buildings could be added as the growth dictated.

It would operate in a business way with leadership that understood the biblical principles necessary to operate a business – or any endeavor- well - a sound investment strategy, organizational principles and strategies that would treat all involved as owners and realize the capability and productivity that inevitably comes when done correctly.

This endeavor could supply many things to a local community and ultimately to outlets in the metropolitan area they border. The beginning objective would be to create something that would be the "go to" place for the local community for food supply and a multitude of other possibilities. As such it would serve as a model for other communities to learn from and likewise create. Ultimately a metro area might be surrounded with such communities and be the ultimate customers of their produce.

A final thought, these communities could also usher in a return to the family based, apprentice oriented development of character and skills that originally drove the American culture. Oh, it might not look quite the same but the result culturally that would accrue could be quite similar to the first 3 centuries of America.

Another final thought, once the concept is proven it could be done anyplace in the country, Imagine a few thousand communities producing goods and services like this. Imagine the opportunities - jobs and the development of new skills for the unskilled, or for young families, or the revitalization of dying communities. The fields are there, the communities are there, and millennial generation, with a little help, is just the generation to make it go!

CHAPTER 12

THE NEW BOTTOM LINE – 2020

Character	Leadership	Economic/Social Dev
Integrated, united self reliant, "can do" Love/pride of country returned Confident	*Excitement re vision High Trust of Gov't "Up from the ranks" "of the people, by the people, for the people"*	*Everyone a stakeholder Entrepreneurial Commom Values/ Direction Individuals/families Prospering*

Is it possible to shift the bottom line like this? It seems like an enormous, rather impossible task. It will be if we try to move it element by element, which would mean many special task forces and special resources provided to those task forces and frankly no one to lead them. Our history is rather dismal regarding this I believe. Organizations of all types want to improve their performance by addressing what is wrong meaning everything that isn't working correctly. That may be the best way for some things but a large organization like our government is too huge to get your arms around. Sometimes (almost always actually) there is a common denominator that, if properly utilized, can be the solution.

Lets go back to the story of Nehemiah. The problem he needed to solve was to rebuild Jerusalem, its walls had been knocked down and the massive gates reduced to ashes. This allowed their enemies to ransack the city at will. There was no order and it was horribly unsafe. The closest thing Nehemiah did in organizing a task force was to take a ride with a "few others" and examine the damage. When he came back he spoke to some "officials" and said simply, "you see the trouble we are in, Jerusalem lies in ruins, and its gates have been burned with fire. Let's rebuild the wall of Jerusalem and we will no longer be in disgrace."

The commentary in the book of Nehemiah in the old testament bible goes on to describe the positioning of the people to work on the wall. He put families on the wall next to their house, shop keepers next to their shop and Priests who needed the gates to work on them. In about 50 days they were finished! I've seen that wall and it was no small task but they were finished! Why? I think it is because of how he positioned the people – he positioned them where they had the most to lose if it was done poorly. By the way, at a point where there was concern that their enemies might try something to thwart work they divided the work force and half of them guarded while the other half continued to work. After the work was completed they had a celebration to Thank God and just bask in their success I imagine.

So the problem was a pretty severe one – their walled city, which as we all know from a school world history class was walled to provide security, it was no longer walled. They had to do something and their attempts to date didn't work. But along comes a leader that thinks differently! He thinks in terms of a common denominator, first the broken down walls but then he thinks about a work force that needs to be mobilized and motivated! Who is going to do the best job fixing a problem on your house? You are, even if you hire someone to do the heavy lifting. You are going to make sure its done right!

So the point is if we can determine such a common denominator we might be able to solve most anything fairly quickly. Sounds good but not that credible? Let me provide another example.

I was given an assignment some years back to restore a manufacturing business. It was a 1950's vintage wood pulp mill. You may have smelled one or two in your life – they sometimes smell like rotten eggs, other times they just smell…bad! I was not happy with the assignment but being a good soldier…I accepted. The pay was good! I knew the story of Nehemiah but was a little perplexed as to how that could help! Also, I had never been in a pulp mill so I had no idea how they worked therefore no idea how to start. Well, Nehemiah took a horse back ride around Jerusalem so it did a similar thing – no horse though. It was worse than I thought. Smelly, rusty pipes and equipment leaking oil; a couple of places where bricks had fallen away from the wall and water everywhere, with oil slicks from the leaky machinery. The mill was about 50 years old and seen its better days for sure but the company was determined to get it running right and for some reason gave me the baton; Punishment for something although I'm not sure what.

Well, we needed to generate some ideas and there were other pulp and paper manufacturing sites in the company that were newer so we organized some teams to visit them and see if we could learn something. There were 6 – 8 to a team and they each went to a different site. I went with the Union committee. All in all we had about 35 people involved – some managers and engineers but mostly what were called "hourly workers". I had been involved in other manufacturing operations and understand that places like this were not your everyday tinker toy assembly line nor were the workers. This was big time industrial America in it waning days and my company wanted to make a bit more money on this one before they called it quits.

So I got to know the guys on the union committee (nope, no women here – this was another place in a time warp), and I found that they were pretty sharp – I developed a respect for what they did and what they knew pretty quickly. I also figured I'd need them to coach me through whatever we needed to do – it wouldn't be the other way around. By the way, I already knew that…I was raised by a journeyman as described in the first chapter.

We returned home and got started with the 35 people that took the trip – they became a design, planning, organizing committee and we worked for about 3 months to develop a line of thinking about the whole operation from how to organize about a thousand people to how to lead whatever that turned into. We also developed a new concept to manage the technical process as well as determining what was needed in terms of equipment - some was worn out and needed to be replaced, other just needed to be updated. I was amazed at how quickly it all jelled and the quality of it all.

By the way this was more than a pulp mill; it sat in the middle of a million acres of land that we managed and cared for, and a pine seedling nursery that grew 25 million seedlings to be planted each year – all in all a pretty big and complicated operation.

There were many aspects to the design but I think the most important one was the pay and promotion system. We designed one that had levels of contribution in return for levels of pay. The contribution was a function of expertise level; ie, the expertise to handle different functions – and the more they could certify in the higher they went. Certification was by a committee of managers and technicians (our word for the workers). Also certification required evidence of being able to do the work usually in terms of a peer and a manager or engineer witnessing the action of doing the function.

There were many other parts of the design of course but this part served as the basis of the union contract we needed to forge. This took another 6 weeks or so but when done we had totally rewritten the contract that had been in effect for years (It had been modified over the years only in terms of pay and benefits – now it was completely different in how the work was viewed; a main shift being from individual "jobs" to roles, levels and teams).

As this was going on the first stages of people transferring to the new system was taking place. Essentially, they were demonstrating what they knew and could do to find the level they would start off and at what pay. Once in the new system they were also eligible and encouraged to learn more and take on more responsibility. This then became the engine of the system. People were highly motivated like those building the Jerusalem wall.

As this was taking place other improvements were being added – new equipment where needed and a totally new approach to managing the process based on "Lean Manufacturing" concepts ("Total Quality" for those who go back as far as I do).

The net effect was a 22% reduction in cost, or about $44 million/year that no longer was being spent…therefore the bottom line improved by that amount. Additionally, the product was better, so higher prices could be charged and the maintenance and efficiency of the equipment was improved making for less shutdowns (in this industry a lengthy shutdown is normally required each year to get inside all tanks and equipment pieces to make sure all in good working order). Because of better maintenance procedures while running this was gradually move to once every 2 years for another big boost in the bottom line.

I may have spent too many words on this but you probably get the idea, the common denominator for me was, and usually is, People. That was true for Nehemiah and it is often true everywhere. When we get that right, and right means motivated people who are knowledgeable about what they are doing. The end result is also good!

That is why the principles used to develop our nations' game plan are so important. From them the road map could be developed that would assure that the people would have a voice and that some would become leaders in terms of being elected to the presidency, the house of representatives, the Senate and, to the federal court system and finally but importantly the same sort of governing bodies in each state.

There was never an expectation or requirement for those roles to be professionalized. The concept was for average citizens to be elected by their peers to these roles. Of course Abraham Lincoln gave strong support this idea in his Gettysburg Address – "that government of the people, by the people, for the people shall not perish from the earth".

We all have a responsibility regarding this, as citizens we have the privilege to cast our votes for those who will lead. If we are not informed ourselves about who those running for the various offices are and how they believe and if we are not aware of what the country needs then we are quite apt to vote poorly or not at all. The way to maintain our culture, our economy, and our security is to vote and to vote in an informed way that puts the people in office who will follow the constitution and will seek to place the right people in the various offices of leadership, the right people being those knowledgeable about the needs of the country and willing to work together with others to seek the best ways to address those needs.

AFTERWARD

The bottom line – *why should I be interested in this business accounting term, It has no relevance to me and what I'm interested in.*

In business the bottom line tells us if we made a profit or not – It is the difference between how much money we made overall less the amount of money it took to make it. If we spend the same amount to make it there is no profit and if we spend more we are losing money – a business can't survive very long if that is the case. The same is true for us as individuals and it is true for our country. Typically, this is about money but we can also think about a bottom line in terms of how we are doing for a wider range of things like the one described earlier; that is, how are we doing relative to our Character, our Leadership and our Economic and Social Development. It can be argued that we are operating at a loss – many of the things we want to be true of our country are not true and haven't been for several years. In business there is a choice, it can change how they are doing the business to improve the product or make it less expensive or both. It is the job of the leaders to determine that and get it moving.

However, we have become a country of professional politicians and business leaders, all who have a personal agenda and probably a chip on their shoulder. In business those leaders are asked to leave if the company is not profitable. But the leaders in our government are allowed to stay as long as they have a constituency that will continue to vote for them to stay – and many do irrespective of how well they work, or don't work with others and irrespective of what their work has accomplished. In fact many have constituency's that want them to strongly appose those who think differently. At best it results in cliques and division that is almost impossible to overcome.

To make this worse there is nothing in our constitution that limits how long a person can serve in the House of Representatives, the Senate and the Supreme Court. The only office with a term limit is the President (the person in this role is limited to 8 years).

You can probably see a problem with this in terms of correcting what is a horrible problem – there are many who view this as a life long privilege and there is no motivation to do a good job, several members sleep during sessions – do you know how that would go down in a for profit company? It could be that the majority of members should enact term limit legislation to correct this but then they would have to leave also at the end of their term, so nothing is done about it – it seems they are preserving this right for themselves! Not the intent of the original congress that put all of this together. I wonder what could happen if "the people" really pushed for this. The first principle the founders worked on was called "Popular Sovereignty" which says that Political Power rests with the people who can alter and abolish government. People express themselves through voting and free participation in government.

I wonder what the origin founders would say about the fact that they didn't spell out term limits and let people sleep through sessions and make no contribution because they have just gotten too old and too unmotivated. I think they would say that this concept of Popular Sovereignty was for things like that – they couldn't possibly think of everything that might require adjustment so they set it up so that the people could – and that process is called voting. We must those in leadership roles know we want this taken care of and make it an expectation that they represent us and do something about it as well as do something about any other obstacle that prevents Congress and the Supreme Court from acting in accordance with the constitution and the Peoples collective will!

In the early days of our country, when the leaders were truly one of the people, I believe it was much easier to find the common ground that was clear, applicable and effective! I see little of that today except in a few business situations and some non profit organizations. Most of the rest of organizational America is weak due to stagnant thinking and frankly wrong thinking.

America started better than that and we have let it erode. It is time for us to take it back and the best way to do that is to vote out the flunkies and vote in some Americans who still believe in America and support its constitution, laws and culture.

www.ingramcontent.com/pod-product-compliance
Lightning Source LLC
Chambersburg PA
CBHW030529210326
41597CB00013B/1077